Don't Shoot the Albatross!

Nautical Myths & Superstitions

Jonathan Eyers

D1142716

For Pat and Brian Eyers

Published by Adlard Coles Nautical
an imprint of A & C Black Publishers Ltd
36 Soho Square, London W1D 3QY
www.adlardcoles.com

Text copyright © Jonathan Eyers 2011
Illustrations copyright © K S Ellis 2011

First edition published 2011

ISBN 978-1-4081-3131-2

A CIP catalogue record for this book is available from the British Library.

This book is produced using paper that is made from wood grown in
managed, sustainable forests. It is natural, renewable and recyclable.
The logging and manufacturing processes conform to the environmental
regulations of the country of origin.

Book design by Susan McIntyre
Typeset in 10 on 13pt FBCalifornian
Printed and bound in India by Replika Press Pvt Ltd

Contents

Acknowledgements

The author wishes to thank Darrel Brown and the members of the Muskegon Conservation Club, Michigan, for their assistance whilst putting this book together.

Note: While all reasonable care has been taken in the publication of this book, the publisher takes no responsibility for the use of the products or methods described in the book. Especially those that involve throwing perfectly good alcohol overboard.

Introduction

If a landlubber scoffs at one of the many superstitions surrounding the sea, he or she should be prepared for at least one salty old seadog to knit his brow, set his jaw and say, 'Ah, but what about the HMS *Friday*?'

During the mid-1800s – so the story goes – the Royal Navy decided to prove there was nothing unlucky about Friday, a superstition on land as well as at sea which made sailors wary of leaving the former for the latter on that day. The HMS *Friday*'s keel was laid on a Friday, she was launched on a Friday, and she set sail on her maiden voyage on a Friday. The Navy had even managed to find a captain named James Friday to command her. Naturally she disappeared without trace before she even reached her first port of call.

Of course, there never was an HMS *Friday*. But sailors remain a notoriously superstitious lot. Some of their superstitions are amusing in their own right, others have fascinating origins, whilst for many there are bizarre anecdotal incidents which would appear to lend some credence to these odd beliefs. This book explores the folklore of the sea in an entertaining but informative way.

There's no point telling a salty old seadog the Royal Navy never named a ship the HMS *Friday*, though. He will already have a response: 'See? Even the Navy is superstitious!'

5

Boatbuilding

Only a landlubber would think a boat is no more than a few carefully put together pieces of wood or fibreglass with a sail up top or an engine behind. A boat is never just a boat. From the time the crew weighs anchor, draws in a mooring rope, raises the mainsail or starts the outboard until the point they step ashore again, the vessel is their home, their shelter, the only thing between them and the fathoms below. And, if things go wrong, she might also be their coffin.

During the Age of Sail, it wasn't only the pressganged ranks of the Royal Navy's warships that were subject to the unforgiving wrath of a brutal higher authority. Centuries before radio, Mayday calls, inflatable life rafts, EPIRB sets and Coastguard helicopters, a life at sea meant a life in the hands of the Gods or fate. Superstitions gave sailors a sense of power – a sense that they weren't completely at the mercy of providence, and that there were things they could do (or not do) to exert some influence over the situations their captains sailed into.

Despite all the wonderful advances in maritime safety and technology, however, we still hear about those who take to the water but never return. So it isn't surprising that the superstitions of old have not only survived, but thrived. They are a tried and tested code of conduct, a religion of the sea. And these superstitions take hold before a boat is even out of the boatyard.

Which wood would be good?

It's easy to imagine the crew of the *Aaron Manby* breaking into cold sweats before her maiden voyage in June 1822. She was, after all, the first iron ship to go to sea. Before then sailors could at least take some comfort in the fact that their ships were built of a material that floats. Though most pleasure craft these days are made of fibreglass, wood has been at the heart of boatbuilding for millennia, so the wisdom of the ages has plenty to offer those who still hanker for a clinker-built craft.

Wood from apple, pear, cherry and elm trees should not be used, though. Before savvy funeral directors started using the much cheaper (for them) veneered chipboard, these woods were used for coffins. There are numerous superstitions that warn against invoking funerals or anything else surrounding death, and in this instance there's a lot to be said for not going to sea in a big coffin. Practically speaking, though, apple trees grow in a twisted fashion that makes the wood unsuitable for construction purposes, and elm decays far too quickly when it goes from wet to dry repeatedly.

Though it makes nice furniture, wood from a walnut tree should not be used in hull construction either. Early settlers in North America were convinced the walnut attracted lightning, whilst many Europeans believed the tree was haunted by witches. It's true that walnut releases a chemical called juglone into the soil, which kills everything from birch and apple trees to tomatoes and potatoes, so the bad reputation must stem from the fact that not much will grow near it.

Oak, on the other hand, was the longstanding wood of choice in shipbuilding, and for good reason. Not only does its timber have great strength and hardness, but the tree has a stellar

reputation dating back to the Ancient Greeks, who venerated it as the tree of Zeus. Its steadfast nature and protective qualities have been celebrated ever since, from early Christians using it to build their churches, to Siberian tribes that decorated oak trees in reindeer pelts and made donations of kettles and spoons to them. Like the walnut, the oak also has a reputation for being struck by lightning, but perhaps because it doesn't kill the spuds too this has been seen as a protective gesture towards us instead.

The ideal wood to build a boat from should be rowan. According to Celtic mythology the rowan is also known as the Traveller's Tree because it protects those on a journey from malevolent forces and prevents them from getting lost. Unfortunately rowan isn't very suitable for building boats; it would take a small forest just to build a little dinghy.

By way of a compromise, however, perhaps a small piece of rowan could be mortised into the hull – but only if it's been pilfered first. Ancient Pomeranians (the Germanic tribe, not the breed of dog) believed a piece of stolen wood embedded into the hull of a boat would help her sail faster, which would be very helpful if the timber merchant worked out where it went.

It used to be the case that a tree growing near to where an unbaptised baby is buried would be inhabited by the infant's spirit. It would also inhabit anything made from the wood of that tree, such as a boat, and protect it. Unfortunately in 2007 the Pope endorsed the International Theological Commission's findings that unbaptised babies may go to Heaven after all. It might just be easier to stick with a fibreglass boat, and try not to try to fall foul of any of the other superstitions in this book.

From keel laying to whiskey plank

Whether the boat is being built out of oak or zinc-anodised steel, the most important date in her construction is the day her keel is laid. The keel is a boat's spine, the backbone from which the rest of her hull takes its strength. If the day she is launched is her birthday, then the day her keel is laid is the moment of conception, and the occasion should be marked accordingly. A good analogy would be laying the foundation stone of a building: the more important the building, the more fuss is made to begin with. If the new boat's owner considers the thing that will keep him from drowning important, he should probably make a fuss too.

In days gone by a priest would officiate at a ceremony to bless the keel, and then everyone would drink. In these more secular times the priest doesn't have to come. But everyone still drinks. A visiting dignitary from outside the maritime community should say a few words, calling on those present to wish the boatbuilders well. When the US Navy lays the keel of a new ship, the dignitary (who is often also the ship's sponsor, see page 26) marks his or her initials on the steel plate that is welded onto the keel first, so that the ship won't forget.

The dignitary who lays the keel should have no vested interest in the boat's future seaworthiness his or herself, lest it seem like pure self interest. With ships being so expensive, this point is often fudged, so that majority shareholders get to lay the keels of cruise liners, and politicians who control defence budgets get to lay the keels of warships. For a new sloop being built in a rented corner of the local boatyard, the dignitary doesn't need to be anyone particularly noteworthy. The landlord of the boat owner's local pub will do; there's always a small chance he'd be sufficiently chuffed at being asked that he might bring the booze for free.

The keel should be laid along a north-south meridian. There's some sound science behind this tradition. A wooden boat being built outside will be unevenly affected by sunlight if she is laid out east-west, so that one side may dry and warp in the sun whilst the other side remains expanded with absorbed moisture. Of course, the theory behind this assumes sunny weather all day, which is why it's probably safer for boats in England to be built indoors. Metal boats should also be built pointing either north or south as they will develop a magnetic field, and a north-south orientation will help that align with the poles. This will minimise the boat's interference with her compass.

As with everything else in the nautical world, the keel must not be laid on a Friday (see reasons why on page 45). Regardless of which of the other six days the keel is put down, once that has been done a French boatbuilders' superstition warns against changing the boat's design. Outside France this is just called common sense.

Making a vacuum-moulded fibreglass hull takes a fraction of the time that it takes to plank a traditional wooden one. Naturally, when the last plank of a wooden boat's hull is put in place, this is cause for celebration amongst those who have laboured long and hard to get this stage. The last plank is known as the shutter plank, because it effectively seals the hull, but more commonly boatbuilders call it the whiskey plank, because they celebrate with a glass of whiskey. The boat's owner can spill a little on the hull if he wants to make an early libation, why not let the liquor flow and let this happen anyway.

Whilst the first nail, bolt or rivet pounded into the hull should have a red ribbon tied around it to protect the vessel from storms, the last one should be made of gold. If most boat owners could afford the gold for that they would probably save a little more and just buy a Sunseeker, so a normal bolt painted gold is an acceptable substitute. Everyone present for the whiskey plank's placing should take a turn at hammering that last bolt in – perhaps before any alcohol takes effect.

Pre-ordering the wind

The laying of the keel is the last time a woman should be allowed to see a boat until construction is completed. However, should a woman accidentally catch sight of a wooden boat during caulking, boatbuilders can demand a 'caulking kiss', which will put things right again. The amorous boys from England's northern shipyards who invented this tradition obviously didn't anticipate future sexual harassment laws, though a woman could escape a kiss by paying the boatbuilder a shilling. A silver coin (rather than a copper-nickel one that only looked silver) would have been better – then they could have put it under the mast.

Sailors' loved ones often hear the palatable explanation for this tradition: that a silver coin placed under the mast during outfitting later buys a fair wind for good sailing, whilst protecting the crew

from storms. Most sailors know that isn't the real reason. The origins of this custom date back to the Ancient Greeks and Romans, both of whom placed a coin in the mouth of the dead. In Greek mythology the dead had to pay the ferryman Charon to take them across the River Styx to the Underworld. A coin in the mouth pays the fare. So does one under the mast. Though one can imagine Charon's reaction to an entire shipwrecked crew hoping to get across on a single ticket.

The US Navy continues this tradition to this day, though with typical pomp and attention to ceremony they mint special coins for the occasion, which are sealed in a box that is welded into the keel instead of below the mast. The masts on modern naval vessels support radio and radar antennae rather than sails, so they aren't stepped through the hull and bedded into the keel. For similar reasons, and proving the adaptability of superstitions, in new motorboats the coin can be placed under the engine mount.

If a sailboat's mast needs replacing, the coin should be retained, but another one added. Some century-old craft sold from person to person have been re-masted, only for the latest owner to discover numerous coins concealed in the mast bed. Though perhaps the original builder was just particularly superstitious. Woe betide anyone who spends a coin found beneath a mast. They might as well be selling their crewmates' souls. Leave it where it is.

As well as a silver coin beneath the mast, Scottish boatbuilders would hide a gold coin somewhere else in the keel to ensure a boat's good fortune. It makes good business sense: no one wants to buy a boat from a boatbuilder whose last craft sank, after all.

Lady Luck (part one)

Nobody ever said superstitions made so much sense that they couldn't contradict each other. The reasons why women should not be allowed on board can be found on page 33. However, many sailors simultaneously believed that women made the best navigators. This was part of the reason why from the mid-1700s onwards the figureheads of large ships usually took the form of a nubile young lady in an otherwise bashful state of undress. Sailors also believed a woman baring her breasts to the elements could shame an angry sea into calming down, which might go some distance to explain why female figureheads became increasingly well endowed. The Ancient Roman historian Pliny the Elder noted the power of female nudity 2,000 years ago, but maybe he'd just been at sea a long time.

Before female figureheads became common, the subject varied. It didn't even have to be human. The Vikings fashioned dragon heads out of the prows of their longships, the idea being that a dragon would scare off any evil encountered at sea; to complete the disguise the stern often tapered to a tail. Elsewhere commanding animals like lions were used. Warships of the Royal Navy often had a soldier in full battle dress, a shield on his arm and a hand on his sword, ready to fight. As with other figureheads, this was meant to embody the spirit of the ship. That was certainly true of some commercial ships too; sometimes the vainglorious owner had an image of himself sculpted onto the front of his vessel – before it set sail to make him even richer.

Regardless of what form the figurehead took, its eyes always had to be open and looking straight ahead. An always-watchful figurehead helped keep the ship's course true, and prevented the vessel from getting lost. In the Mediterranean sailors painted an eye on the bow of their boats for the same reason. Modern sailors who can't fit a big wooden figurehead on the front of their Hobie 33 could also try this. The eye mustn't be painted green, as this is the colour of the land, and suggests a boat is looking for shore because she isn't happy at sea. No part of a boat should be painted blue either; this is the colour of the sea, and the gods might lose sight of a little blue vessel in thousands of miles of open ocean. Alternatively, modern sailors wary of getting lost at sea could invest in a good GPS system instead.

Burning your boats

Some boatbuilders, particularly of traditional wooden boats, claim a boat has a personality which becomes apparent as she is put together. Working on them day after day, boatbuilders can tell whether she's going to be docile and obedient to her crew, or whether she's going to fight them and need taming. The most intricate of wooden boats may contain several hundred separate parts, which all have to fit together, and then work together. A boat that rejects parts could be proving herself tenacious or even mulish. Of course, the boatbuilder may just be passing the buck for his own shoddy workmanship. But as recently as the twentieth century, vessels that left the boatyard with a bad reputation have been burned rather than launched. Their reputations preceded them, and crew refused to sail in them.

One final warning: whilst a boat is being built, never mention her name within hearing distance of her. Wait until the official christening. She knows what her name will be before her owner does. If she hears it she may wake up before she's actually ready to.

Naming and Launching

Amongst all the other superstitions surrounding boat names, the most obvious one is often missed: the practice of naming a boat in the first place. Apart from teenage boys, not many people name their cars. Indeed, it would make more sense to identify a boat with a unique registration number or code, like cars have, especially in a busy marina where there are already three yachts called *Seas the Day* and four called *Aquaholic* (two perennially popular boat names, at least in the US).

But *D690VEV* sounds rather cold and clinical, and is certainly not romantic. No part of the boat's spirit or personality is captured, hence giving her a name. Far from referring to her as a vehicle or machine, a name resembles a living thing, and acknowledges her role and importance. She is not just a beast of burden or a form of transport, she has responsibilities toward her crew and passengers, to protect them from threats at sea.

So a new boat's owner must choose a name carefully. A boat may reject a name she doesn't like, and misfortune will plague any attempts to sail her. Remember, too, that many sailors are wary of changing a boat's name. Nobody wants to own a boat named after another man's wife, for example, so the name could be the deciding factor whether an unwanted boat gets sold to a new owner, or rusts in a corner of the boatyard.

No monkey business

Avoid wry, suggestive names that the boat may live up to. American senator Gary Hart learnt this the hard way. He was a rising star of the Democrat Party in the 1980s and was considered the frontrunner to challenge the first George Bush for the Presidency in 1988. As soon as he announced has candidacy, the tabloids started digging up rumours suggesting he had cheated on his wife, and might still be doing so. Hart boldly challenged the media to follow him around, declaring that he had nothing to hide. Not long after, photos appeared in the press of him relaxing on a yacht, his arm around 29-year-old model Donna Rice, who was sitting on his knee. The yacht's name was *Monkey Business*. Hart dropped his candidacy a week later.

Also avoid conceited names that might tempt fate. Names like *Queen of the Seas* or *Storm Rider* may cause the Gods to think, 'We'll see about that.' During the golden age of Britain's maritime supremacy the Royal Navy gave many ships audacious names, such as *Conqueror, Victory* and *Invincible*. Rather than strike fear into the heart of Britain's enemies (particularly the French), this proved to be great folly. The HMS *Conqueror* launched in 1758 sailed for only two years before being wrecked on the approach to Portsmouth in 1760. A century later, in 1861, another HMS *Conqueror* ran into a reef in the Bahamas and sank in less than 30 feet of water.

She had only been launched a few years previously, too. Neither vessel did much conquering in their short lifetimes. And whilst the HMS *Victory* was victorious at the Battle of Trafalgar it should be remembered that Admiral Nelson never came home from the battle (except pickled in a barrel of brandy, see page 57).

However, ships named *Invincible* appear to have roused the ire of the Gods most. One ship named HMS *Invincible* ran aground and sank in the Solent in 1758. Heavy winds drove another ship of the same name onto rocks off the East England coast in 1801; it then ran aground on a sandbank and 400 crew drowned, despite the proximity to shore and two vessels that came to her aid. In 1914 yet another HMS *Invincible* sank, in a storm off Portland Bill, and this one was perhaps triply ill-fated, given that she was a battleship in a class designated Audacious, and she had also been renamed (see page 27). The worst fate befell the HMS *Invincible* that served as her squadron flagship during the Battle of Jutland in 1916. Two German ships sank her in just over a minute. One salvo hit her magazine and the resulting explosion tore the ship in half. Of the 1,032 people on board, only six were pulled from the water alive.

Sticks and stones…

Finding a suitable name for a boat is made harder by the fact that whilst there are plenty of rules about what a boat can't be called, there is precious little advice about what she can be. Don't name a boat after a reptile; they are land animals that don't take well to water. Don't name a boat after mythological beasts like sea monsters with the intention of making her seem formidable. It is very bad luck to name a boat after something that may harm her. This category also includes fire, lightning, tsunamis and women (see page 24). Don't name a boat after a strong wind, like *Scirocco*, or a storm, like *Cyclone*. It won't make her sail any faster, and associates her with something most sailors would probably rather avoid.

Naming a boat after a person *is* acceptable – depending on who it is. Ideally it should be someone who is strong but not a challenger to the power of the gods, courageous but not reckless, swift but not rash. So few boats should be named after the owner's wife. Naval heroes are particularly good namesakes. Naming a boat after one honours them, and indicates the boat aspires to share their attributes, and hopefully their success. A Royal Navy ship named HMS *Nelson* laid down in 1814 passed through several owners' hands and went through various conversions but retained the name until she finally went out of service – 112 years later. Four other vessels named in honour of Admiral Nelson have also had long, successful careers.

Names containing seven letters are meant to be lucky. Unfortunately this wasn't the case for the SS *Sultana* in 1865, during the final weeks of the American Civil War.

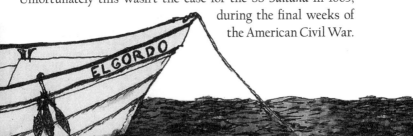

The paddlesteamer, which had a legal capacity of less than 400, was transporting 2,400 soldiers who had been liberated from prisoner of war camps in the Confederate South. Three of the *Sultana*'s four boilers exploded, destroying part of the ship and turning the rest into a raging inferno. With the ship so hopelessly overcrowded, 1,800 of those on board died. It remains the worst maritime disaster in American history. A seven-letter name didn't help the *Sultana*, but that might be because the name also broke a different rule, which suggests bad luck is more powerful than good luck.

The letter A

The idea that it was bad luck to give a vessel a name ending in the letter A spread swiftly and widely during and after the First World War. Perhaps the most infamous nautical disaster of the war was the sinking in May 1915 of a ship with just such a name: RMS *Lusitania*. Torpedoed by a German U-boat, the cruise liner sank in under 20 minutes – long enough to save only 700 of the 1,900 people aboard. In contrast, when the *Titanic* sank three years earlier it took two and a half hours, which would have been long enough to rescue all of the *Lusitania*'s passengers – she was only 8 miles off the coast of Ireland when she was attacked, after all.

The *Lusitania*'s name may have proved unlucky for those on board, but the sinking did help turn the happily isolated American people against the Kaiser, precipitating America's entry into the war and Germany's subsequent defeat. Less than 48 hours before the Armistice was signed, however, a battleship that had survived the entire war was sunk off Cape Trafalgar, and became the last Royal Navy vessel to be lost in the conflict. Her name was HMS *Britannia*.

The US Navy also has a history of officially scoffing at this particular superstition. It prefers instead to honour revolutionary America's first major victory over the British in 1777 by repeatedly naming vessels after that particular campaign: the Battle of Saratoga. However, no less than three ships to bear the name USS *Saratoga* have met ignominious ends. The first *Saratoga*, launched in 1780, was lost at sea less than a year later, and still has not been located to this day. Another sank in December 1941 (and perhaps they were asking for trouble with this one, given that they'd also changed her name, see page 27). Yet another *Saratoga*, one of the country's first aircraft carriers, was sunk by an atomic bomb test in 1946.

To give the US Navy due credit, it deliberately scuttled the *Saratoga* in December 1941 to prevent it falling into the hands of the Japanese. The *Saratoga* that later fell foul of the A bomb had been left near to the blast intentionally (only 500 yards away, in fact) to test the effects of an underwater detonation on America's warships. She took a perfectly noble seven and a half hours to sink. Nothing untoward has befallen another three ships to bear the name USS *Saratoga*. The last, commissioned on President Eisenhower's orders, was still in service when President Clinton came to office, forty years later.

Triskaidekaphobia

Another unlucky letter is M, but in this case it is unlucky for boat names to start with it. In 1838 the SS *Moselle* was considered the finest steamship on the Ohio River, the largest tributary of the Mississippi. The Cincinnati press lauded her as the fastest steamship yet built, an accolade that may have gone to the head of her twenty-eight-year-old captain, who allegedly tried to race another vessel. A massive build-up of steam in her boilers caused

an explosion so strong that debris landed on shore almost half a mile away. Two thirds of those on board died.

M is unlucky because it is the thirteenth letter of the alphabet. Triskaidekaphobic sailors won't give a boat a name with thirteen characters either, nor will they leave port on the thirteenth day of the month, especially when that falls on a Friday (see page 45). The superstition that the number thirteen is unlucky abounds on land as well at sea. Nobody knows for sure where it came from, but it has been around for thousands of years. The Ancient Persians believed the twelve constellations would each control the world for 1,000 years, and at the start of the thirteenth cycle the world would end. In the Norse pantheon, the thirteenth God was Loki, the troublemaker, and the number thirteen is particularly significant in Christianity, because there were thirteen diners at the Last Supper, with the thirteenth usually held to be Judas Iscariot. Twelve witches make up a witch's coven, with the thirteenth place reserved for the Devil, whilst the thirteenth card in a Tarot pack represents death.

Lady Luck (part two)

Given that the fairer sex bring bad luck with them if they're allowed on board (see page 33), it would be unwise to name a boat after one, as it's then impossible to escape any ill fortune that besets her because of it. Naming a boat after an engaged woman is even worse; it will make the boat jealous.

Despite this, every kind of nautical craft from a little dinghy to an aircraft carrier is always referred to as 'she' even if, like HMS *Churchill*, they are named after a man. As a former First Lord of the Admiralty, the man himself would have understood why: a life afloat being fraught with so many dangers, sailors view their vessel as a sort of protective mother figure looking after her children.

Modern linguistics experts claim this isn't the origin of the tradition, however. As any high school student could point out, in other languages, such as French, gender has a grammatical role, and boats take the feminine form (*la boat*, for example). In Old English, which was a lot closer to European languages, gender also had a grammatical role, and this may have been retained with regard to boats and ships as the modern language developed.

In these times of increased sexual equality, some have suggested abandoning the practice and calling boats 'it'. But so far there is little sign sailors have abandoned superstition in favour of political correctness.

Why boat owners like cava

A boat must always be christened, and the ceremony must take place before she hits the water. A boat owner who tries to christen his craft after she's already afloat won't shake the ill fortune he brought upon himself by not doing it in the first place.

Boats are christened for essentially the same reason that newborn babies are: to formally introduce the vessel to the Gods, to call on their blessing, and to ask them to protect her from evil. Priests sprinkle holy water on a baby's forehead; boat owners smash a bottle of champagne against the bow. It is very unlucky if the bottle fails to break. However, the rumour that the bottle failed to break during the christening of the *Titanic* is actually false. In fact, the White Star Line, who operated many cruise liners like the *Titanic*, never christened any of their ships, much to the chagrin of their more superstitious employees. In 2007 the bottle did fail to break when Camilla, Duchess of Cornwall, launched the Cunard liner MS *Queen Victoria*. On one of the ship's first major cruises nearly 100 passengers were struck down by the norovirus, the winter vomiting bug.

Though the Ancient Greeks launched a new vessel with copious drinking (and the inevitable spills), the modern tradition of offering a libation apparently began with the Vikings. The

ceremony may have grown more grisly as the story spread amongst the Vikings' nervy enemies, but the Norse warriors supposedly marked the launch of a new longship with human sacrifice. Prisoners tied to the slipway were crushed as the vessel slid into the water; their blood helped grease the skids.

Boat owners in more civilised times found perfectly adequate substitutes for blood. Red ribbons tied around the nails on the slipway served that purpose. Red wine, which symbolises blood in many Jewish and Christian traditions, even looked the part. Eventually, however, champagne replaced red wine because it was seen as more prestigious, and more celebratory. Given that the difference between blood and champagne is quite significant already, new boat owners counting pennies after forking out for boatyard fees could be forgiven for opting for cava instead. And unless they want to be back in the boatyard for more work pretty quickly, they would be best advised not to smash any glass against a fibreglass hull, too. Shake, then spray.

As with laying the keel, a priest used to officiate at the launch, blessing the vessel and announcing her name, but the priest's attendance is no longer mandatory here either. Royal Navy ships and notable British liners like the *Queen Victoria* are often launched by members of the Royal Family. Vessels of the US Navy and Coast Guard usually have a ship's sponsor to launch them, typically a female civilian who may also have laid the keel. The role calls upon her to be a sort of ship's mascot, though she is regarded as a permanent member of the crew – even if most of her crewmates probably wouldn't want her to join them on board (see page 33).

'What a ship was christened, so let her stay'

So says Long John Silver in chapter eleven of *Treasure Island*, as he describes the grim fates suffered by the crews of ships that had been renamed. Changing a boat's name after she's sailed has long been considered unlucky. During the Age of Sail it was difficult to find crew willing to work on renamed ships, which carried bad reputations even if nothing untoward had happened to them.

One of the most famous ships to change name and meet a sticky end was the *Endurance*, the ship Sir Ernest Shackleton took on his ill-fated voyage to Antarctica in 1914. Her Norwegian builders christened her *Polaris*, but Shackleton renamed her in honour of his family motto: 'By endurance we conquer.' A week-long gale in the Weddell Sea turned slushy floes into pack ice, trapping the beleaguered *Endurance* hundreds of miles from safety. Worse was to come, because despite a reinforced hull the ship was slowly crushed by compressed ice, and eventually sank. Remarkably, every member of her crew did eventually get back to England, but they spent two years marooned on the ice first.

Renaming a boat may appear like an attempt to sneak past the gods, affect a disguise to escape their attention, avoid retribution for past misdemeanours, but deviousness like this won't go unnoticed, or unpunished, even if the unwitting boat owner renamed her out of vanity rather than guile. A proper renaming ceremony makes a transparent and open appeal to the gods to acknowledge the boat's new name, showing that there is no ulterior motive.

There are various ways to go about this (every clique of sailors has its own favoured method) but all of them should make the owner of the local off licence happy. If possible, the boat should be hauled out of the water, and the ceremony conducted when the hull is dry. The first step is to obliterate all traces of the boat's old name, wherever it can be found. The logbook and any other paperwork with the boat's name on must be burnt. The ashes should be scattered into the sea (or lake, river, canal, etc). At this point some sailors would go even further, and re-mast the boat, burning the old one. The boat's name on the stern must be scratched off, not just painted over. If she's a seagoing craft, cleanse the hull with fresh water. Ask the gods (and ask nicely) to forget the boat's old name. Then go through the christening process again, using whiskey. Give the first tot to the water, the second to the boat, but be sure to have enough left for everyone to toast the new name.

And that's the least outlandish way to rename a boat. Another technique insists the boat be scuttled with the old name, then raised with the new; this is the expensive option. Another requires the owner to sail the boat backwards for a nautical mile, reversing over the old name; this is the difficult option. Yet another suggests it's as simple as getting a virgin to urinate over the bow; this is the disgusting option. One optimistic father (who clearly doesn't read the papers) got his teenage son to do it.

Of course, many sailors don't believe renaming ceremonies work, and that they just anger the gods further with the presumptuousness of it all. For those who do believe in them, there's one cardinal rule: once a boat has been given a new name, never mention the old one again.

Before Casting Off

To the sailor who remains unconvinced by superstition, the hours before departure are for victualling, paying any outstanding marina fees, and showing off to people whose ten year old Beneteau 331 looks decidedly grubby next to a brand new boat. But for everyone else, this is a period demanding extreme vigilance.

Sailors who cruise to parts of the Caribbean are often warned about the risks of mooring in local marinas, and some who have done it advise others to take advantage of a marina's watchman service, if available. A boy will sit and guard the boat (for a price, of course) whilst the owner stretches his legs ashore. Most sailors would find a similar service very handy in their home port, too. Before setting sail there are so many people to avoid, things to keep off the boat and bad omens to look out for that it's usually too much for a single sailor to do by himself.

Meanwhile, wish a sailor who's sceptical of superstitions good luck before he casts off. He'll need it, but he won't get it. Some people need to learn the hard way.

Good luck is bad luck

It's fairly well known that actors think it very bad luck to be wished good luck before a performance, as it could form a contradictory curse and bring them bad luck instead. Many sailors believe the same is true if someone wishes them luck before they set sail, but there is no nautical equivalent to the actor's alternative, 'break a leg'. A sailor never wishes another good luck unless he doesn't really mean it. Fortunately, the bad luck can be reversed by spilling a little blood. The person who wished a sailor good luck in the first place can provide it; a prompt left-hook to their nose or lip should get it.

There are numerous pre-departure rituals sailors can observe to reinforce the good luck that should have been bestowed upon the boat during building and launching. Reiterating the libation performed at both keel-laying and christening, a little wine should be poured on the deck. As if sailors needed any more reason to stock up on alcohol, another toast should be made immediately before leaving port (see page 49).

Sailors from Lunenburg, Nova Scotia believe docking on the east side of a wharf brings a vessel luck. Alternatively, when only the west side is free, carrying fire around a boat renews her luck. Health and safety officers at the marina will stop pushing their pens around for a moment to protest about that, so less incendiary gestures include touching the bow first thing in the morning, spitting over the port side, or spitting on a coin and then tossing it overboard.

In the past, fishermen from Dorset attached stones with holes through them to the bows of their boats. These holy (in both senses of the word) flints were the same kind of lucky stones, called hag stones, that people would hang up outside their front doors to protect their homes from witchcraft. At the beginning of the fishing season fishermen would also 'salt in' their nets, blessing them and sprinkling them with salt, beseeching the sea to provide a good catch this year.

Get a tattoo...

Tattoos have been a sailor's trademark for hundreds of years. The crews of ships exploring the Polynesian islands in the eighteenth century observed how the natives did it, and brought the practice back to Europe. A few lucky sailors may have got their tattoos put on by experienced Polynesians; most got one from a crewmate with a knife and some ink. Given that tattooing became a popular below-decks past time, as was drinking rum, this was obviously an exercise best not attempted in rough seas. Sometimes tattoos were given to commemorate a sailor's achievements, such as a turtle standing on its hind legs to signify a sailor had crossed the Equator (see page 59 for more about the line-crossing ceremony). An anchor, meanwhile, signified a sailor who had crossed the Atlantic.

An anchor tattoo was also thought to protect a sailor from drowning, an idea which probably arose because those who had crossed the Atlantic must have seemed blessed to survive the journey. Similarly, swallow tattoos were lucky because a swallow always finds its way home, but a sailor was only permitted to get a tattoo of one once they had travelled more than 5,000 nautical miles. Perhaps the sailors who originated this tradition were worried anyone who hadn't already proved themselves a good seaman might ruin the plausibility of the superstition. Sailors who had yet to travel 5,000 nautical miles could get a tattoo of a compass rose or a constellation of stars used in celestial navigation.

31

Sailors who hadn't crossed the Atlantic but wanted a tattoo to protect them from drowning could get a pig tattooed on the top of one foot and a rooster on the other. Despite pigs being bad luck to have on board (see page 82) and unmentionable at sea (see page 55), both pigs and roosters are notoriously afraid of water. Put a pig or rooster in water and it will find the quickest route back on to dry land.

Other recommended subjects for tattoos include a naked woman, which has the same ability to calm storms as a ship's figurehead (see page 14). Getting 'HOLD' tattooed across the knuckles of the right hand and 'FAST' across the knuckles of the left helps a sailor hold onto ropes, particularly rigging. A crucifix tattooed on the sole of each foot will stop sharks from biting (though a shark bite might be less painful). A crucifix tattooed on the back, on the other hand, reduces the pain of a flogging. But not many a sailor would want to crew on a boat where he'd need that one these days.

...or a piercing

Seeing as sailors are not meant to take money on board (see page 40), a gold earring ensures the wearer will always have something of value on them. Traditionally sailors wore a gold earring in case they died in a foreign port, because the earring would cover the expense of giving them a funeral. Indeed, Scottish law supposedly once required local fishermen to wear one so that if a fishing vessel sunk, any bodies that washed ashore could pay for their own burial – assuming opportunistic beachcombers didn't get to them first, that is.

Ear piercing is at least 5,000 years old. The world's oldest naturally mummified body found frozen in the Ötztal Alps on the Austria-Italy border (popularly known as Ötzi the Iceman or Frozen Fritz) had pierced ears, and he died around 3300 BC. Ancient tribes believed earrings prevented evil spirits from entering the body through the ear, a belief that endured at sea as well as on land for thousands of years. Sailors came to see earrings as a charm that protected them from drowning, too. They also believed a pierced ear improved the eyesight in the opposite eye, hence why many got both ears pierced. This idea is corroborated by traditional Chinese medicine – the ear lobe has various acupuncture points for treating eye problems.

Like tattoos, earrings also commemorated a sailor's achievements. Sailors got a new piercing in the left ear to mark the occasion when they crossed the international date line, the Arctic Circle, the Antarctic Circle or the Equator (see page 59). Meanwhile a black pearl earring (or in more recent times, a brass one) signified a sailor who had survived a sinking ship. So he could be considered either blessed for surviving or jinxed for sinking in the first place, depending on how his crewmates saw it.

Lady Luck (part three)

Of all the people who should be avoided before setting sail, and who should not be allowed on board either, top on the list come women. Women should not come down to the dock to see a boat off. In fact, it's bad luck for a woman to even pass a man on his way to the boat. More obliging women in less egalitarian times would turn away, go home or hide if they saw a sailor heading in

33

the direction of a harbour. Some fishermen's wives didn't do any washing on the day their husbands set sail in case this evoked a fishing vessel taking on water and sinking. At least, that was the excuse they gave their superstitious husbands.

For a long time it was probably in women's best interests to stay on dry land anyway. If anything untoward happened at sea, women on board often found themselves the scapegoats. And if disaster struck, desperate sailors sometimes took drastic action.

In 1387 Sir John Arundel led a campaign in France, halfway through what became known as the Hundred Years' War. Returning to England the following year his fleet was caught in a terrible storm off the Cornish coast. Twenty ships were lost, and a thousand men drowned, including Arundel himself. There were less than ten survivors, who revealed that, as the ships foundered, panicking crewmen threw more than sixty women overboard, hoping to placate the tempest. When they heard about it, the French thought the storm divine justice; whilst waiting for a good wind to sail back from Brittany, Arundel's man had taken refuge in an abbey, where they had gone wild with the defenceless nuns before looting the place. Some reports suggested the women thrown overboard were in fact nuns that Arundel's men had abducted.

Obviously the idea that a woman could calm a storm by baring her upper body to the elements hadn't appeared by the late fourteenth century. Either that or maybe the nuns were thrown overboard because they refused to do it. Regardless, this is one of several contradictory superstitions about women at sea. Another says it's lucky (for the boat) for a child to be born on board, whilst another says that a bride who steers a boat on her wedding day will give the vessel protection from storms.

The more cynical of maritime historians believe the superstition against women at sea was fostered by shrewd captains who didn't want them on board – and who found a cunning way to make their otherwise lustful crews not want them on board either. On a 200ft–long ship with 800 crew there wasn't room for anyone incapable of the physically demanding work. Women would serve only as a distraction so by turning women into walking bad omens, captains ensured the crew wouldn't want them anywhere near the ship either, even on an almost mutinously long passage between ports. Of course, if it was a captain who invented the idea that a woman on board makes the sea angry, it was probably his equally shrewd crew who invented the idea that a naked woman can calm it again.

These days women serve in both the Royal Navy and the US Navy on all kinds of vessels except submarines, which don't have space for separate facilities. Some of these ships have run into trouble, but most haven't, and there's no evidence (lawsuits, out of court settlements, etc) that a female crewmember has ever been called upon to undress on the fo'c'sle.

Priests and other Jonahs

Maybe Sir John Arundel's men got the idea of throwing women overboard from the Bible. The story of Jonah appears in the Koran and the Jewish Tanakh too. God ordered Jonah to go to the city of Nineveh and spread His word to its wicked citizens. Instead Jonah fled, seeking passage on a ship heading in the other direction. This being the fire and brimstone God of the Old Testament,

He wreaked a terrible storm upon the ship. At first the sailors threw cargo overboard, to no effect, but when they discovered Jonah sleeping below decks he told them what he had done, and suggested they throw him overboard too. When they did, the storm dissipated. Meanwhile Jonah was swallowed by a great fish (only modern cetologists have identified it as being a whale).

Needless to say, anyone called Jonah (or one of its variant forms: Jonas, Jonasco, Yonas and Yunus) is unlucky to have aboard. Even if it isn't his name, a sailor who previously sailed on a vessel that suffered some misfortune, or whose arrival on board coincides with any unfortunate incidents, may also be referred to as a Jonah. Like the women on Arundel's ships, a Jonah is a convenient scapegoat to blame for a downturn in luck. However, some other sorts of people are considered Jonahs before they even leave shore, so shouldn't be allowed anywhere near the boat, and should be avoided before setting sail too.

After women, the pre-eminent Jonahs are priests. A boat's christening is the last time a priest (of any faith or denomination) should have any contact with her. Many superstitions are about not angering the gods, but having a priest on board may attract the malevolent attention of the Devil too. A priest is unlucky because one of his main duties is to perform funeral rites. Just as having an empty coffin aboard evokes a funeral (see page 39), the presence of a priest suggests a crew are ready for one. Those who are prepared for a death at sea may get one – or more. It's unlucky to wear black clothes when sailing, and this probably arose because priests traditionally wear mostly black. Similarly, it's unlucky to let a lawyer on board in case they are mistaken for a priest; apparently in days gone by lawyers wore a lot of black too. In fact, anyone wearing black on the dock before a boat sets sail is a bad omen. So perhaps the worst type of Jonah is actually a nun: a woman, wearing black, linked to a priest.

Cross-eyed, flat-footed or red-headed people are unlucky to have on board. People with flat feet are considered unlucky on land as well, but during the Age of Sail sailors believed their flat-footed crewmates were more likely to fall from the rigging. The Ancient Egyptians held red-heads to be untrustworthy and potentially duplicitous, a belief that later appeared amongst Christians too; Judas Iscariot is thought to have been ginger. Neither the flat-footed or the red-headed are quite as bad omens as women or priests are, however. Indeed, a sailor who passes someone with flat feet or ginger hair on his way to the boat can avoid bad luck simply by speaking to them before they speak to him. A few choice words should make it clear they aren't welcome near boats.

Contraband

Ideally, the security employed at the dockside should be as rigorous as the security employed at an airport. Just as plane passengers have to submit to metal detector gates and wands, and their luggage passed through an X-ray machine, anyone boarding a boat should be searched for items that may prove dangerous. This is made easier for the most superstitious of sailors, who believe any form of luggage is bad luck, and won't let anyone bring anything on board. Others believe only black

bags or suitcases are unlucky. Black is the colour of death, whilst suitcases evoke a coffin. On a related note, if a passenger tries to bring an empty coffin on board with them they should be stopped at the gangplank (if not sooner). An empty coffin is nothing but an omen that before the voyage is out someone on board will fill it.

Similarly, flowers should not be brought on board because they are used for funerals, and their presence suggests the crew is anticipating one. Flowers can be used to make a wreath, after all, and they are an omen that someone on board will die. If any are found after leaving port, throw them overboard and hope they were found early enough. In fact, any sort of plant (including their seeds) has no place at sea. Roots seek the earth; whilst on passage the closest earth is usually the seabed, and the quickest route is straight down – through the hull. Actually, it's probably safest that nothing green be taken on board either, green being the colour of the land.

Other things not to allow on board include an umbrella – a sailor who expects bad weather may get it. Don't even risk a sun parasol on a nice day. Sailors should throw any money they have in their pockets overboard before they set sail. The sea will not reward anyone who doesn't appear to need it. This applies particularly to fishermen, whose catches will be small if they're carrying cash. Balls of wool were thought to be used by witches when performing spells, so whilst it's unlucky to find some on board, it's even unluckier to take some on board intentionally. The same applies to sewing needles and pins, which may cause the boat to sink. A whitethorn stick is unlucky on any journey;

take one made of hazel instead – according to an old Irish superstition, hazel had power over the Devil.

The caul of a newborn

Whilst there are plenty of things that will bring bad luck to a boat, the luckiest charm to have on board is the caul of a newborn. Unfortunately that's only slightly more helpful for the nervous sailor than telling him hen's teeth are lucky. It's very rare for babies to be born with a veil over their face because the amniotic sac usually breaks during labour, though notable figures to have been born with one include Sigmund Freud, Lord Byron, Liberace and possibly Jesus. Dried or smoked, the caul was believed to protect the bearer (who needn't have been born with it himself – he could use someone else's) from drowning, so naturally they became prized by sailors from the Middle Ages onwards. Over the centuries sailors attributed other benefits to bearing one; as well as being a general good luck charm, the caul supposedly also made navigation easier, or at least more accurate.

Poor parents whose newborn was born with a caul could certainly expect an upturn in fortune, if only because they could demand a high price for it from sailors and fishermen. Advertisements offering cauls for sale appeared in British newspapers, with an advert for one appearing in *The Times* as late as the 1840s. Often these sales went to auction. Charles Dickens wrote about such an auction in *David Copperfield*, the eponymous hero of which was born with a caul, and is present at the auction where it sells for 15 guineas. However, David is unimpressed, noting: 'Whether seagoing people were short of money about that time, or were short of faith and preferred cork jackets, I don't know.'

During the Age of Sail, sailors who had acquired a caul would present it to their captain in the hope its protection would extend to the ship and her entire crew. A sailor who was born with one was of course considered very lucky, whilst a landsman born with one would probably want to keep a low profile when the press gangs of the seventeenth and eighteenth centuries were in town. The widespread belief in the luck of a caul prevailed into the twentieth century. Liverpool's Merseyside Maritime Museum has the caul of sailor James Fairclough, who was born in 1913 and who kept it with him throughout his naval career, during which he survived several torpedo attacks. In fact, to this day cauls still occasionally show up on online auction sites.

Nobody knows when the superstition originated, but some historians have suggested the cloth diadems of Ancient Roman leaders were meant to evoke a caul, so as a symbol of divine protection and authority the caul has been around for millennia. Early Christians, however, denounced the superstition, though later, with the pagan connotations expunged, some Christians believed the caul was cut from cloth worn by Jesus Christ, symbolising His protection. This belief clearly didn't travel as far as Poland and other countries in Eastern Europe, where people believed a child born with a caul would invariably grow up to become either a werewolf or a vampire.

Other lucky luggage

The sailor who is outbid at the last moment for that caul on eBay needn't fret, because there are plenty more things they can take with them to bring them luck, and most are more readily available. Salt, for example, is considered particularly lucky at sea, and is in plentiful supply these days. In the Middle Ages, however, it was a precious commodity, regarded as a pure substance, and venerated for its medicinal uses. Before antiseptics and disinfectants, physicians recommended salt for cleaning wounds, reducing swellings, treating burns and controlling allergies, amongst other things. Its reputation as a cure-all (and a great way to improve a bland supper) must have elevated salt to such an esteemed position that many sailors believe to part with salt is to part with luck. Spilling it is worse than giving it away, though. Judas Iscariot supposedly spilt salt at the Last Supper (Leonardo da Vinci depicted this in his version, but the area beneath Judas's hand has been worn away over time). If any salt is spilt, some should be thrown over the left shoulder immediately – this is where evil spirits (or even the Devil himself) lurk.

Other lucky charms (varying in their availability) include turtle bones, shark teeth, eagle beaks, pieces of fur (or the tail of a fox), and the feather of a wren slain on New Year's Day, which will protect the bearer from being shipwrecked. Every galley should have a rolling pin, and a glass one if possible. Meanwhile a horseshoe nailed to the mast will help the boat avoid storms. Scottish fishermen also believed that nailing a right boot they had caught by mistake to the mast would bring them good luck. A left boot, on the other hand, should be thrown back immediately (see page 93).

Setting Sail

With so many rules to adhere to even before the anchor is weighed or the lines cast off, it's a surprise the most superstitious of sailors don't just pack in this boating lark and take up golf (where failure to wear a red shirt or carry three pennies won't result in drowning). Unfortunately for them, the superstitions affecting boat construction, launching, naming and preparation are only the beginning, and it's when the mainsail is hoisted or the outboard started that the rules really become paramount.

The degree of forward planning involved, especially regarding the specific dates available to leave, and departure procedure, might make it seem like setting sail entails as much fuss as launching a space shuttle. Astronauts, however, don't need to worry about which foot they should use to step aboard their vessel.

Paraskavedekatriaphobia

To the superstitious, the sailing week has only six days. More so than people on land, where Friday also carries unlucky connotations, sailors have long been wary of setting sail on that day. Many believed no good would come of any venture begun on a Friday. Fortune would abandon anyone who tried. No fish would be caught. It was the day when the sea was at its cruellest, and the gods at their least merciful. In a nutshell, to set sail on a Friday was to risk life and limb (and boat).

The superstition is popularly held to have originated from the fact that Christ was crucified on a Friday. However, that's not the only ominous appearance of Friday in Christian theology. It was apparently also on a Friday that God both expelled Adam and Eve from the Garden of Eden, and sent the rains of the Great Flood, from which only the Bible's best sailor (and his menagerie) escaped. So it's perhaps not surprising that early Roman Christians insisted Friday be held as a fast.

Friday also had negative connotations outside the Abrahamic religions, though. In English, German and Dutch the day is named after the ancient love Goddess Frigga (also known as Freyja), who in the pantheon of Norse gods is equivalent to Venus. She is Odin's (allegedly) cheating wife. With their natural suspicion of troublesome women, many sailors would surely be wary of a day named after one. In Norse mythology Friday was also the witches' Sabbath. Meanwhile, even Brahmins in India, exposed to neither Western religion nor Norse paganism, warned that nothing new should be started on a Friday.

Whilst any Friday is bad, the worst is of course one that falls on the thirteenth day of the month, which happens at least once a year. The fear of Friday the 13th has been catchily named paraskavedekatriaphobia. The reasons why the number 13 is unlucky can be found on page 23, and combined with the reasons why Friday is already unlucky, that makes Friday the 13th doubly unlucky. Some historians believe that the date got its negative connotations because on Friday 13th October 1307 the King of France, Philip the Fair, ordered the Knights Templar arrested and tortured for confessions of heresy, for which they were subsequently tried and burnt at the stake.

Though Sir Robin Knox-Johnston missed the 13th, he still set out on the *Sunday Times* Golden Globe Race on a Friday. As told in his account, *A World of My Own*, he left Falmouth in his yacht *Suhaili* on Friday 14th June 1968. Friday certainly didn't prove unlucky for him. After 312 days alone at sea (and despite suffering appendicitis whilst he was out there) he arrived back at Falmouth on 22nd April 1969, becoming the first person to sail single-handedly around the world non-stop. He received a CBE from the Queen for his achievement, and was later knighted too. None of the other eight sailors who took part (including Bernard Moitessier, Chay Blyth and Donald Crowhurst) finished the race.

The superstition against Fridays may have been around for hundreds if not thousands of years, but it grew in popularity amongst sailors during the nineteenth century as Britain's naval might increased. It is statistically likely that sooner or later something bad will happen on a Friday, or on a voyage that set sail on a Friday, and Britain didn't get to be the greatest naval power in human history by operating on a six-day week. Fridays (even ones that fall on the thirteenth day of the month) are, statistically speaking, no more unlucky than any other days. It's just that people don't pay as much attention to the other days, or other combinations of dates.

Other bad dates in the sailor's calendar

Whilst the law of statistics may 'prove' there are no especially unlucky days, if a superstitious sailor is expecting misfortune, he may just get it. In Ghana, for example, fishermen won't take to the water on a Tuesday, because tradition allows the fish a day to rest. Fishing every day of the week is unlucky, because those who try it would be considered greedy by the gods, and wouldn't catch any fish. Tuesday can also be an unlucky day in Spain, where Tuesday the 13th is just as bad as Friday the 13th. Spanish Christians believe Tuesday the 13th was the date of the Last Supper and the day when the Romans arrested Jesus Christ. It's bad luck to marry or go to sea whenever Tuesday falls on the 13th, regardless of the month.

Sailors of a Christian leaning should also avoid sailing on other dates that coincide with infamous happenings in the Bible, such as 31st December, which is the day Judas Iscariot hanged himself. As well as Fridays and Tuesdays, some Mondays should be avoided too. The first Monday in April is the date of the first murder, when Cain slew his brother Abel, whilst the second Monday in August is the date God destroyed the decadent, vice-ridden cities of Sodom and Gomorrah.

The word 'dismal' comes from the Latin phrase *dies mali*, which essentially means 'evil days'. In medieval times people commonly believed certain dates to be inherently unlucky, that nothing should be undertaken on those days, and that any journey begun, whether by land or by sea, was imperilled. Political correctness not being quite so common back then, these days were often called Egyptian days. The Saxons held there to be 24 evil days in the year, but by the reign of Henry VI in the fifteenth century this number had crept up to 32. January is the worst month, with seven evil days (the 1st, 2nd, 4th, 5th, 7th, 10th and 15th), whilst October is the best month with only one (the 6th).

Sunday sail, never fail

So, there are plenty of days when it's unlucky to sail, but precious little advice about when it's good to go. Sunday seems the safest bet, despite being the day of rest in the Christian tradition, because Jesus Christ was resurrected on a Sunday. It's not uncommon for the captains of modern merchant vessels to request a Sunday departure. They're not pandering to superstitious crews, however – Sunday simply tends to be a lighter day at sea. As for specific dates, the 17th and 29th of any month are apparently good days to set sail on a long voyage.

How to board properly

Anyone boarding a vessel for the first time should ask the captain permission to come aboard, but failing to do so will only prove unlucky if he's a stickler for courteous convention – and he's the one with the key to the drinks cabinet. Otherwise, the most important thing to remember when stepping aboard is to lead with the right foot. Stepping aboard with the left foot first is unlucky (and sneezing to the left at the same time the worst luck of all), particularly amongst Christian sailors, many of whom believe the left side is where evil lurks (hence throwing salt over that shoulder – see page 43). Christ is always depicted using his right hand, especially to baptise people, whilst Satan is depicted using his left hand to do the same. In Islam, too, the left hand also traditionally has negative connotations, to the extent where it's very rude to proffer it for a handshake. Whilst fishermen consider a right boot to be lucky (see page 43), they regard a left boot as very unlucky, and anyone who catches one accidentally should throw it back immediately. As well as boarding with the right foot first, sailors should step off the boat the same way if they ever want to sail her again.

How to leave port

The last (necessary) thing to do whilst still moored is to toast the gods. Open a new bottle of whiskey, ensure everyone on board gets a tot, and then empty whatever is left in the bottom over the side. If anyone has brought an old pair of shoes with them, this is the point to throw them overboard to ensure good luck on the voyage. Those going fishing, meanwhile, should empty their pockets of any money (see page 40) if they want to catch any fish. Don't allow anyone on the dockside (or on board) to throw a stone near the boat as she is about to set sail, especially if the stone will land in the water. This is a sign of disrespect to the sea and angers the gods, and will ensure the vessel never returns (thanks to the inevitable stormy weather and huge waves heading her way in retaliation).

Apart from that, providing every rule up to this point has been followed to the letter, it should now be reasonably safe to weigh anchor or cast off. However, there's more to leaving port than just avoiding daysailers chartered by people whose moveable ballast was bottled in the south of France. Never watch a loved one go out of sight. This applies equally to those on board, leaving people behind, and those on shore, waiting for the boat to disappear over the horizon. There's no surer way to guarantee they're never seen again. Don't call back to someone on the dock, and make sure they know not to call out to the boat once it has pulled away from the wharf, too.

A sailor should never look back once he has left port. It suggests to the Gods (and his crewmates) that he is not ready to leave the land. Others on board will see the unsure sailor as a bad omen, who will attract misfortune to the boat. If anything happens, he's bound to be identified as the Jonah (see page 36) – and he'll deserve it.

On Passage

Britain's most famous lexicographer Dr Samuel Johnson once said, 'No man will be a sailor who has contrivance to get himself into a jail. For being in a ship is like being in a jail – with the chance of also being drowned. A man in a jail has more room, better food and commonly better company.'

It wasn't too irreverent an opinion for a learned liberal gentleman of the eighteenth century, when a life at sea in the Royal Navy was only noble in the misty eyes of land-based warmongers, romanticising their disputes (usually with the French) for the benefit of the public who were paying for it all. For the sailor, the only time he wasn't a slave was when he got shore leave. Between ports, any expression of dissent came at a price – thirty six lashes of a cat o' nine tails from the boatswain's mate in front of the entire crew gathered on the poop deck.

Obviously things have got a bit better since then, but a captain should still keep a close eye on everything those aboard his vessel do and say, regardless of the size of the boat and the number of people sailing her. One person could bring calamity down upon everyone else without even knowing it.

Things not to do on board

Harbourmasters may be officious, but they are kindly uncles compared to the Gods, and once a boat passes the breakwater she is in the gods' jurisdiction. The most important thing not to do after leaving one port is to talk about the next. A sailor who talks about his destination as if taking it for granted that he will get there risks displeasing the Gods. It's very presumptuous to assume the boat is safe from the wrath of the sea en route, and talk of where she is going may tempt the Gods to prove otherwise. Don't even count the number of nautical miles left to go; don't refer to such distances in definite terms. A sailor should talk only of headings, not destinations. It's fine to be trying to get there – he should just be aware that it's at the discretion of the gods if he ever will.

On a small boat there are usually more important things to worry about than a pedicure. However, male sailors should also be aware that the archetypal salty sea dog doesn't just wear a beard to make himself look rugged and manly. Cutting hair (including a beard), fingernails or toenails is forbidden whilst on passage. Invariably the cuttings will end up in the sea. In Ancient Roman mythology these were considered offerings to Proserpina (known as Persephone in the Greek pantheon), but the sea being Neptune's kingdom, these offerings to her would make him jealous. As usual, his response took the form of a deadly storm.

In more modern times, sailors believed that if the sea got a taste of them, it would be hungry for more, and they would be living on borrowed time (see page 58). For the same reason if a sailor cut himself or pricked his finger on a needle (or fishhook) he was careful not to let any blood drip into the water. He could wipe it on the sails instead, as getting blood on them is lucky. Some sailors also believe that cutting their hair on a rising tide will give them a cold.

Doing anything that invokes the boat capsizing and sinking is obviously not a good idea. Unfortunately the ways of doing this unintentionally are legion, and they might be seen as bad omens by others on board (see page 36). Sleeping on the stomach was a lot harder to do when sailors had to sleep in hammocks slung between cannons; in a cosy berth in the forepeak of a modern yacht it's a lot easier to roll over without waking up. As well as sleeping the right way up, sailors should ensure neither shoes nor loaves of bread are ever left upside down. Teapots should never be upturned to empty them either. Indeed, some sailors believe a teapot should never be emptied at all, and will keep on topping it up with fresh water and new tea bags. Don't spit in the hold of a vessel, as this invokes the hold filling with water. Don't stick a knife in the deck – this is a disrespectful act which threatens the hull's integrity.

There are plenty of other things a sailor should not do, but the reasons why (and where these superstitions came from in the first place) have been lost to history. Never strike a nail on a Sunday. Don't leave a broom lying on top of fishing nets. Don't pass a flag through the rungs of a ladder, and don't repair a flag on the quarterdeck either. Don't stir a pot or wind a rope counter clockwise. As well as sleeping the right way up, a sailor should make sure he never sleeps with his head toward the bow too. Despite on-board toilets being called heads because they were traditionally situated in the bow of the ship, it's unlucky to throw any waste off the head of the boat and then pass over it. Perhaps this one arose because someone fell in whilst leaning out too far, had the ship go over them, and invariably drowned in their own muck. That would inarguably be one of the unluckiest ways to die at sea.

The sailor's thesaurus

At sea even more than on land, words have power. Some are like invocations, and mostly of bad luck. Of the many words that should not be uttered on a boat a lot of them refer to people, animals and things that are unlucky at sea in themselves. Sailors and fishermen from the Isle of Man, on the other hand, believe it's unlucky to refer directly to any animal that has hair on its body. However, many of these forbidden words have acceptable alternatives for use on a boat – some of them are obvious nicknames, whilst others seem like a sailor's secret code.

Cat – 'scraper' (Isle of Man), 'nose shaver' (Shetlands)
Church – 'the steepled house'
Dog – 'moddey' (Isle of Man)
Deer – 'hart' (though this is a medieval term referring to stags older than five years)
Drown – 'go to Davy Jones's Locker', 'go for the long swim'
Egg – 'roundabout'
Fox – 'the red-eared one'
Goodbye – a sailor should never say anything of the sort if he ever wants to see that person again (likewise a landlubber should never say it to a sailor)
Hare – 'mauken', 'long ears' (can also be used to refer to a rabbit, though hares generally have longer ears)
Knife – 'sharpie'
Minister/priest – 'capstan', 'sky pilot'

Pig – 'grunter', 'grumphie', 'turf rooter', 'curly tail' (or just spell it out)

Rabbit – 'bunny', 'pommits' (Isle of Man), 'underground mutton' (western Britain)

Rat – 'uncle' (Isle of Man), 'long tail' (or 'lang tail' in Scotland)

Rope – 'line' (using 'rope' will supposedly awaken the spirits of the hanged)

Salmon – 'red fish', 'beastie', 'the gentleman'

Salt – 'white stuff'

Though in the interests of avoiding possible harsh consequences, it's probably safer to ignore this last one when declaring to Customs officials. Afterwards, as when any of the other words are mentioned by mistake, touch wood or invoke cold iron (see page 95) and hope misfortune passes by.

Medicine at sea

The popular impression of maritime medicine usually precludes anything more successful than a wooden peg leg or an eye patch. However, this does a disservice to the fine homeopathic tradition that has developed amongst sailors over the centuries. Rheumatism, for example, can be cured by laying the hand of a drowned man on the affected limb. If a drowned man isn't available, red herrings should be rubbed into the area instead (though this may not be as effective as a drowned man's hand).

Eels are something of a nautical wonder drug. Eating eel can cure a fever, whilst powdered eel liver can cure deafness. In parts of Scotland and Northern Ireland, sailors believed fresh eel skin could cure cramp too. Meanwhile a sailor with toothache should carry a small piece of flesh cut from a dogfish that has been returned to the sea alive. If anything made of iron on board

gets rusty, the rust can be used to treat gout. Should someone on board impale themselves with a fishhook they should stick the hook into a piece of wood to speed up the healing process. It would be very unlucky to try and use it to catch any fish, given that no blood should be allowed to fall into the sea (see page 53).

Death on passage

During the Age of Sail, death at sea was a common occurrence. Though sailors feared tempestuous weather more than anything else, storm-driven sinkings accounted for only a minority of fatalities. Even amidst the pitched sea battles between the fleets of the European empires vying for maritime supremacy, it wasn't cannon fire that killed the most men. Of the 100,000 British sailors who died during the Napoleonic Wars, only 1,500 died in action. Whether in war or in peace, the number one killer of sailors was disease, which killed 60,000 of those 100,000 men who died in the fight against France. To put that in a contemporary context, despite remaining the second largest naval force in the world today, the Royal Navy only has 60,000 personnel in total. The worst killer was typhus, which was spread by lice. If one sailor came aboard carrying infected lice he could infect the entire crew, even if not infected himself.

According to sailors' lore, the spirits of those who die at sea can spend the afterlife in Fiddler's Green, which has all the benefits of a rowdy tavern (endless music and dancing, bottomless tankards of rum) without any bills (or hangovers) to bear. Unfortunately getting into Fiddler's Green requires fifty years of service at sea. Even if they joined at 12 or 13, which wasn't uncommon at one time, most sailors during the Age of Sail would have had to have been very lucky to live long enough. Today, also, most personnel in the Royal Navy retire by the age of 55. So most sailors who die at sea probably end up in Davy Jones's Locker instead, a considerably less desirable final resting place at the bottom of the sea, where barnacles grow over the hulks of sunken ships and the bones of those who once manned them.

After Admiral Nelson died following victory at the Battle of Trafalgar, his body was stripped, shaved and squeezed into a barrel that was then filled with brandy for transport back to London. It might not seem like a fitting end for Britain's greatest naval hero, but he received better treatment than any of those who died under his command. If a sailor died his corpse was placed in his hammock, with cannon shot at his feet to make sure he didn't float. The sail maker sewed up this makeshift body bag, putting the final stitch through the nose. Supposedly this was to ensure the sailor was really dead, not just very drunk (and heading for thirty six of the best from the boatswain's mate). Bodies were disposed of quickly. Funeral services lasted only a few minutes, with officers not allowing them to interrupt the ship's routine. Crewmen slid the body overboard on a plank (though superstition insisted this mustn't happen parallel to the line joining bow and stern).

Perhaps a shrewd captain invented the superstition that it was bad luck to keep a body on board to ensure his crewmen would want to be rid of their friend without too much fuss. Sailors often believed a ship carrying a corpse would sail slower, and that the souls of the dead might linger around any body that hadn't been given a proper burial (whether in the earth or beneath the waves). Friends or not, spirits brought trouble to a vessel. Late in 1952 the trawler *Thornella* brought seven bodies back to Scotland from a wreck off Greenland, but was caught in hurricane-force winds that destroyed the bridge. And in the days before refrigeration, a quick dispatch was just common sense.

Unfortunately, modern legal protocols provide very little leeway for the superstitious sailor. What he might view as a burial at sea the authorities would probably look upon as someone dumping a body without obtaining a death certificate. And that's usually only done by murderers trying to get rid of the evidence. Unlike the HMS *Victory*, most (though possibly not all) yachts don't carry enough brandy to pickle a body, so the deceased should be returned to port as soon as possible. En route, make sure his or her eyes are closed. If a dead sailor's left eye remains open, they will find someone to take with them. However nice the deceased's clothes are, nobody should wear them on the same voyage, or bad luck will strike the vessel. On eventually reaching port, it's unlucky for anyone to disembark before the body is taken off.

In times past, a sailor's attitude towards death seemed to be to give a nonchalant shrug and just get on with things. There were so many ways to die at sea – and most of them beyond any individual sailor's control – that it didn't bear thinking about. Few sailors bothered learning how to swim. They believed the sea got to decide who sails on it, and who lives and dies. They also believed that what the sea wants, the sea will have. So there wasn't much point learning how to swim. Notably, a blue vein across the bridge of the nose apparently makes someone susceptible to drowning (unless they were born on a Sunday, in which case they are fine). If someone fell overboard, most sailors wouldn't make much effort to rescue them. Believing that once the sea gets a taste of someone it will be hungry for more, sailors considered someone who fell in but survived to be living on borrowed time. His crewmates expected the sea to come searching for him, which meant everyone on board was at risk. Many wouldn't even retrieve an item of clothing that fell overboard for the same reason. That said, some sailors (especially in wartime) believed a stranger saved from drowning could turn their enemy.

Crossing the line

Of all the coordinates on the map that require special attention from those sailing past, the most eminent is the line at latitude 0 degrees. There are 25,000 miles of it that can be crossed, with the majority of it at sea. To sailors, the Equator is more than just the invisible boundary between north and south. It is the point when the ocean becomes a strange alien place, where everything starts going backwards. Winter comes in June; the sun travels along the northern edge of the sky; even water goes down holes in a different direction – and storms spiral the other way too. European sailors, used to it being at the heart of celestial navigation, lost sight of the North Star. So naturally, crossing the line has great significance to sailors, and deserves proper acknowledgement. Many sailors saw the need to beseech the Gods for further protection, hence the tradition of toasting Neptune.

As described in her account, *Against the Flow*, record-breaking circumnavigator Dee Caffari toasted Neptune with champagne and chocolates as she crossed the Equator in 2006. She asked for safe passage heading south. It turned out to be the most gruelling leg of her round-the-world journey, so on her second approach to the Equator, heading north again, she planned a special tribute. Once again she gave the sea champagne and chocolates, but this time added a photo of her father, the man who introduced her to sailing, and whose death was the spur for her adventure. Neptune was clearly pleased. The rest of her journey went much more smoothly, and she went on to sail into the record books as the first woman to sail single-handedly around the world non-stop – against the prevailing currents (something only four men had managed before her).

Historically, many of the world's navies made a lot more fuss, with a ceremony held on deck involving the entire crew. The French were first to hold some sort of ceremony to acknowledge crossing the Equator in the sixteenth century, but the British Royal Navy soon followed. The assembled crew was split between those who had crossed the line before (known as trusty shellbacks, or just shellbacks) and those who hadn't (known as slimy pollywogs, pollywogs, or just wogs). Sometimes the ceremony involved staging a mock royal court before an officer dressed up as (and representing) Neptune. The shellbacks brought the pollywogs before him to ask him to grant them permission to cross the Equator with his blessing.

This was the nice ending to an initiation rite that often began the day before with a series of brutal trials for the pollywogs that would today be classed as abuse. Shellbacks could make pollywogs suffer a gauntlet of humiliations, which at their most innocuous included shaving the hair off the pollywogs' bodies or making them crawl through rotting food scraps. Crueller shellbacks would beat pollywogs with salt-encrusted ropes or hoses, throw them over the side and drag them behind the ship, or, as recently as the late twentieth century, prod electrified pieces of metal into their naked flesh. Polish pollywogs got off lightly by having to eat an uncooked egg; Norwegian pollywogs had to drink a shot of diesel fuel. This kind of thing was still going on in the Australian Navy as late as 1995, when a leaked video of pollywogs being sexually assaulted on a submarine whilst officers watched made it onto the nightly news. Unsurprisingly there are rumours of deaths resulting from shellbacks getting too carried away. Of course the Royal Navy and the US Navy have now banned any such brutality, but rather than drive it underground, some US Navy officers have turned it into a quaint traditional ceremony instead.

From a shellback's perspective, the severe treatment was designed to make the pollywog fully appreciate the significance of crossing the Equator. The pain and humiliation (and day of vomiting, for those Norwegians quaffing diesel fuel) was a fair price to pay for Neptune's blessing. There were special classes of shellback, too, for those who crossed the Equator at the Prime Meridian (a Royal Diamond Shellback in the Royal Navy, or an Emerald Shellback in the US Navy) or at the 180th meridian – the International Date Line (a Golden Shellback). Plus, looking at it from the other angle, any pollywog who was conferred as a shellback could look forward to visiting the same treatment upon any other pollywogs who joined the crew in future.

The Bermuda Triangle

Another area sailors (specifically those in the western Atlantic) should mark on the chart is the most infamous of no-go zones – the Bermuda Triangle. Unfortunately nobody can quite agree where it is, or how big an area it covers. By the largest estimation, the

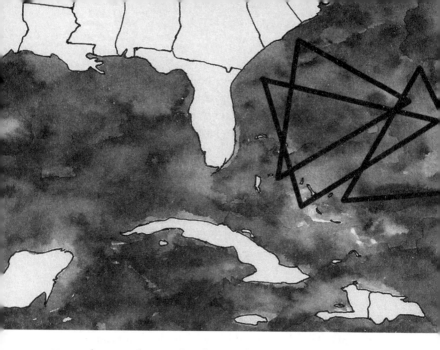

Bermuda Triangle stretches from as far up the eastern seaboard of the United States as the border between Virginia and North Carolina, to the coast of Venezuela in the south, and as far east as the Azores. Generally, however, most people assume it covers an area from the Florida Straits in the north, far enough south to include all of the Caribbean, and far enough east to include Bermuda.

Despite supposedly having a longstanding reputation for mysterious disappearances, most of that reputation has been generated retrospectively, with ships and boats that vanished in the past explained away by this all-encompassing theory. The concept of the Bermuda Triangle first appeared in a 1950 magazine article, and didn't get its name until another article in 1964. It originally gained notoriety not because of a ship's disappearance but because of the disappearance of an entire squadron of US Air Force planes on an exercise over the Bahamas late in 1945. All five Avenger torpedo bombers of Flight 19 vanished without trace, with the squadron leader's last radio messages reporting they had no idea where they were. Another plane sent out to search for wreckage or survivors also disappeared without trace, an unlikely twist that probably cemented the Bermuda Triangle's reputation.

Over the years countless incidents have been attributed to supernatural forces at work in the Bermuda Triangle, even when there have been reasonable explanations, and when those incidents could just as easily have happened elsewhere too. The Bermuda Triangle is blamed for the disappearance of Joshua Slocum, for example, who was heading from Massachusetts to Venezuela on *Spray* in 1909. His route would have taken him straight through the Bermuda Triangle, though nobody knows exactly when his voyage met its end. As the first man to sail single-handedly around the world, he was obviously highly experienced, so the mystery surrounding his disappearance has helped propagate the idea of malevolent forces being behind it.

The US Navy has lost several ships in the area, including the collier USS *Cyclops* in 1918, which continues to represent the largest loss of life the US Navy has suffered in a single incident not involving combat. Though the presumption there is that the *Cyclops* wasn't sunk by a German submarine. The same cause has been attributed to the disappearances of the USS *Proteus* and USS *Nereus* during the Second World War. However, in both conflicts U-boat commanders kept logs of every vessel they attacked, and none of these ships appear in any. All three, however, were of the same class, built at the same time. There was only one other ship in the class, and that three of them sank might suggest some common design flaw.

In 1921 the schooner *Carroll A Deering* ran aground on rocks off North Carolina on its way north from Barbados, and when boarded by would-be rescuers, was discovered to be completely abandoned. In the galley they found food half cooked, as if the cook suddenly stopped in the middle of preparing it. The excitable Bermuda Triangle theorists of the 1950s and 1960s latched onto this as the classic story of a ship's crew vanishing in the area. More sober analysts suggested piracy could be involved. The crew disappeared during Prohibition, when rum-running was rampant between the Bahamas and the American mainland. Perhaps the *Deering* was a smuggling vessel, or the crew were killed by smugglers from another ship. The Bermuda Triangle area was popular with pirates between the sixteenth and eighteenth centuries too. The most famous pirate of all, Edward Teach (popularly known as Blackbeard), operated in the vicinity, and it's probable the area retained its bad reputation from then.

Regardless of the specific points where the corners of the Bermuda Triangle are located, the area remains one of the busiest shipping zones in the world. There is a considerable amount of commercial shipping between North and South America, and between both and Europe. The Caribbean is also one of the most popular destinations for cruise liners – and pleasure boaters from Florida too. But it's also an area notorious for tropical storms, and the Gulf Stream runs straight through it. The strong current could carry away boats that were drifting after losing engine power or sails. Just as Fridays are not statistically more likely to be unlucky (see page 45), neither is the Bermuda Triangle. It's just that people pay more attention to disappearances which occur there. It remains unlucky, however, to cross any area where another vessel has sunk, wherever that is.

Signs and Portents
at Sea

Modern sailors are spoilt. Christopher Columbus, Ferdinand Magellan, Marco Polo *et al* didn't have pilot atlases with little arrows showing them the direction of prevailing currents, or hurricane tracks. Whilst most of their contemporaries didn't sail more than a few miles from a coastline, the pioneers of maritime exploration set a course to the perpendicular. They were sailing into the unknown with a guy up the mast instead of radar. Nowadays sailors have access to weather forecasts too, and can remain in contact with home via satellite at all times. Even in dangerous waters, far from land, sailors can know roughly what to expect and can be prepared.

Being prepared has always been on sailors' minds, and the best way to be prepared is to know what's coming in the first place. People have been trying to (or claiming they can) predict the future for thousands of years. Supposed methods have developed all over the world, from reading how tea leaves lie in an emptied cup to anthropomancy – divination using the entrails of a disembowelled man. Sailors had to learn how to read signs at sea. The gods have long provided plenty of indications of how things will go, whether in the form of bad omens, mystical visitations and visions, signs in the sky or the behaviour of animals.

Unhappy accidents

All kinds of things can happen
on board that a sailor should take as
a warning. For example, finding a penny is
one of those superstitions that means the reverse
of what it means on land – especially for those
fishing (see page 40). The sea won't reward those who
don't need money, so a fisherman should throw a found
penny overboard.

If someone cleaning the deck loses a bucket or mop overboard
then that is a sign the vessel is heading for misfortune.
Likewise, losing a hat over the side, perhaps caught by a stiff
breeze, signifies a long trip (sailors should not try to reclaim
it, see page 58). Hearing a hatch fall into the hold

is another omen of bad luck, whilst seeing a
hatch replaced upside down means someone
on board has doomed the boat to sink. A
wine glass ringing of its own accord is also a
sign that the boat might sink; it sounds like a
church bell. Stop it before it stops ringing on
its own.

The bells, the bells

In the Middle Ages people believed bells could keep away evil
spirits, which were scared off by the sound. Special hand bells,
called dead bells, were even baptised, and the recently bereaved
shook such a bell over the body of their loved one to prevent
evil spirits from attacking before a proper Christian burial
ceremony could be carried out. Bells have come to be associated
with funerals, which means, like everything else associated

with funerals, the sound is bad luck at sea. A ship's bell ringing of its own accord foretells that someone on board will die. This superstition probably arose because a ship's bell is most likely to ring on its own in gale-force storm winds, when everyone was at risk. Whilst anything that sounds like a ship's bell ringing is also a bad omen, this only includes the bells on buoys or other navigation aids if the sailor doesn't want to be near land – and therefore possibly rocks. A bell embodies the soul of the vessel, and will ring both when she is wrecked, and from beneath the waves at the spot where she sank.

St Elmo's Fire

One omen that sounds like it should be mythical but is an actual atmospheric phenomenon is St Elmo's Fire. Appearing as a blue or violet glow, often accompanied by a hissing or buzzing sound, St Elmo's Fire is usually seen flickering around the top of a mast. It's not actually a flame, of course, but luminous plasma discharged from a grounded object in an electrical field. That's the same kind of electrical field which builds up before a thunderstorm, and can cause someone's hair to stand on end.

St Elmo's Fire has appeared to sailors throughout history. Its appearance was noted in Antonio Pigafetta's record of his voyage with Magellan to the Indies, and by Charles Darwin aboard the *Beagle* in South America, who wrote: 'Everything is in flames... even the very masts are pointed with a blue flame.' Sailors on the British vessel *Charles Bal* saw multiple lights on the masthead and yardarm in 1833 when they were several miles away from Krakatoa as it erupted. Major volcanic eruptions often cause an electrical field to build up in the atmosphere, hence why eruptions are often accompanied by lightning, even without a storm.

The significance of the phenomenon to sailors dates back at least two thousand years, with references appearing in the writings of Julius Caesar, Pliny the Elder and Seneca. Roman sailors apparently thought of the lights as Castor and Pollux, the two gods who protected those at sea. To modern sailors St Elmo's Fire can be either a lucky or an unlucky omen. If the glow remains high upon the mast, it is a sign that the worst weather is behind, and the outlook looks good. However, if the glow appears around a man's head, it means he will die within a day. There is some scientific backing to this. Sharp, pointed objects require a lower voltage level to produce the effect of St Elmo's Fire, so if the glow appears around someone's head, the electrical field must be quite considerable. He or she could soon become a human lightning conductor.

St Elmo's Fire is named after St Erasmus, the patron saint of sailors, who was martyred by being disembowelled and having his entrails wound round a windlass (which might explain why he is also the patron saint of intestinal problems). He supposedly kept preaching after lightning struck the ground beside him. Many sailors consider the glow a sign of his protection, as if he is holding a candle over the vessel. According to some sailors, one flame means bad weather is coming, whilst two flames means the weather is clear. Actually two separate discharges means a greater electrical field has built up around the boat, which probably isn't a good sign.

The Flying Dutchman

Of all the things a sailor might see on the horizon, the worst (even worse than fast-approaching storm clouds) is the terrifying spectacle of the *Flying Dutchman*. This has a scientific explanation too, even if it isn't quite what the legend suggests it

is. As far as sailors are concerned, the *Flying Dutchman* is a ghost
ship manned by a dead crew and commanded by a captain who
defied the gods. So there's a warning to all sailors in that. The
Flying Dutchman can never go home, doomed to sail the oceans
forever. She is usually spotted from far away, sometimes glowing
with an eerie red or green light, and sailors consider her a portent
of doom. Misfortune promptly besets any crew that sees the
Flying Dutchman. Sickness, starvation, insanity and death soon
follow. Nobody who sees the ghost ship will ever see land again
(which doesn't quite explain how word of its significance spread,
if everyone who saw her swiftly died).

The *Flying Dutchman* is the English nickname for the vessel. Nobody knows what she was actually called. Historians, humouring the superstitious, have posited several real Dutch ships and captains the legend may have been based upon. Her skipper may have been Bernard Fokke, a seventeenth century captain celebrated for his speedy trips between Europe and Indonesia. Apparently, he was so intent on driving his ship (and his men) ever faster to make more money that he made a deal with the Devil. Another possible captain is Hendrik van der Decken. He supposedly tried to sail his ship around Cape Horn, which is famous for its heavy winds, strong currents, large waves and treacherous icebergs. When the ship got into difficulties, van der Decken started cursing God and firing his gun into the wind. Though other versions of the same story locate it off the Cape of Good Hope instead.

According to the most plausible scientific explanation for sightings of the *Flying Dutchman*, she is more likely to be seen near Cape Horn because it's colder there. The phenomenon of Fata Morgana is most commonly seen in polar regions, though the North Sea can be sufficiently icy at times to explain the prevalence of sightings in the area. Fata Morgana is a phenomenon similar to a mirage, where an atmospheric 'duct' between a distinct layer of warm air over cold air acts like a refracting lens. This causes radiation (such as light, or radio signals) to bend and follow the curvature of the earth, rather than head in a straight line off into space as usual. So what sailors see floating just above the sea on the horizon is actually a ship just out of sight beyond it. There would surely be more sightings, but if there isn't a ship in the right place at the right time, sailors would see only sky appear above the waves (which they probably wouldn't even notice).

Weather

Even if they were at greater risk from not washing their hands before they ate, what sailors during the Age of Sail feared the most was storms. Given that superstitions developed as a way for sailors to try and influence that which was beyond anyone's control, it's perhaps not surprising that the fear of inclement weather inspired some of the most desperate suggestions – such as baring a woman's naked upper body to the elements in an attempt to calm a tempest.

Now that sailors are less ignorant about hygiene (and typhus is virtually unseen outside of the Tropics), bad weather can justifiably be a sailor's number one concern. Countless books offer advice about heavy weather sailing. Few of them suggest pouring oil on troubled waters. Whilst oil might help stop waves breaking to a certain extent, it could require a sizeable slick only a major multinational petroleum company would be capable of providing (and they tend to only do that accidentally). Instead, learn how to read the signs that foretell coming weather, and avoid doing anything that might anger the seas.

Red sky at night, sailor's delight

Before industrialised farming, this was more of a shepherd's superstition, hence the more common appearance of 'shepherd' rather than 'sailor' in the rhyme. Though the rhyme itself originates from Britain, the observation dates back at least two thousand years. It features in the Bible, appearing in Matthew 16:2–3 as a warning to the Pharisees and Sadducees not to ignore signs from God. Unlike many superstitions, this one has a basis in scientific fact, though it is more likely to be an accurate gauge of developments in the weather in temperate regions, and where weather comes over an ocean to the west. A red sky at night means the skies are clear and there are no big clouds to reflect the red end of the sunlight spectrum as the sun sets in the west. However, the rhyme usually concludes: Red sky in morning, sailor's warning. As the sun rises in the east, a red sky means the red in sunlight is reflecting off big clouds to the west. These clouds won't necessarily develop into a storm, of course, but it means there is an increased risk.

Another sign of rain is a ring or halo around the moon. This also has a scientific explanation. Ice crystals in the upper atmosphere cause the appearance of a ring by refracting moonlight, and an increase in temperature could turn those ice crystals into water – rain. Some superstitious weather-watchers also believe that the number of stars they can see within the ring indicates the number of days until they can expect rain. A new moon also divides sailors as to its meaning. Some believe if the crescent of a new moon appears horizontally, that means the next month will be dry, whilst others believe the opposite, that a horizontal new moon presages dry weather. Regardless, if it starts raining, pay heed to another rhyme: Rain at seven, fine by eleven. In most parts of the world it doesn't get hot enough for more than four hours' worth of rainwater to be evaporated in one go.

Whistling at sea

Don't take any form of recorded music on a boat. Not because it is unlucky in itself, but because people might start clapping or whistling along with it. Just as clapping at sea is bad because it brings thunder, whistling at sea summons up a storm. The wind sees (or rather hears) it as a direct challenge, and will not back down from that.

Whilst accepting that whistling when the wind is already blowing will turn a breeze into a gale, some sailors insist a soft whistle can attract a gentle wind when stuck in the Doldrums or other becalmed seas. On ships in the past only the youngest boy was allowed to do the whistling, on the assumption that his lungs weren't strong enough to whistle up a storm. Other sailors believe in cutting a small hole in the mast and whistling quietly into it for a useful wind, and then sticking the knife in the mast to hold it when it comes. Plenty of sailors maintain any whistling is dangerous, and that, the wind being in the mast in the first place, sticking a knife into the wood is all that's needed to release it. No whistling required.

Those exempt from this ban in the past of course included officers, if they needed to give signals or commands to the crew when their voices wouldn't carry or orders had to be given quickly. That said, many sailors used to be fine with the cook whistling, too – if he was whistling they knew he couldn't be helping himself to their rations down in the galley.

Selling the wind

Rather than whistling for wind, a sailor could try buying it in advance. At some point in the Middle Ages, business-savvy witches in Britain or Europe came up with the idea of selling wind to sailors. Often what they sold were charms, such as short

lengths of rope with three knots tied in them. Witches in the Finnish part of Lapland wouldn't give sailors a charm, but sold the promise of a spell, claiming they would know if the sailor needed wind and could summon up a gust remotely. Enough people held these witches responsible for the plentiful winds at sea that selling wind grew into something of an international trade by the end of the sixteenth century. The last wind seller in Europe, however, was Bessie Miller from the Orkney Islands off Scotland, who sold wind for sixpence a time in the nineteenth century.

Alternatively, a sailor who knows he is heading toward the Doldrums (or other parts of the oceans where he might need a little help behind the sails) should take a black cat with him. If he needs wind, he can lock it in a chest or cupboard, and it will stir up a stiff breeze. He shouldn't keep it in there for long, though (see page 81).

Animals

It's not hard to imagine what it must have been like below decks on Noah's Ark. Besides the fact most of the menagerie (the female half, anyway) probably left the ship pregnant, at least the human passengers used the heads. During the Age of Sail, large ships on long journeys carried livestock to provide fresh meat. Some warships also transported cavalry horses. Space being at a premium, animals and crew usually slept within scratching or biting distance of each other.

With the filth, the smell and the noise, it's no wonder sailors developed an aversion to many animals. Most of these superstitions appeared in the last few centuries. After all, assuming there's something literal to the story of Noah, he must have taken two of each species on board his boat, but there's nothing in the Bible about rabbits or pigs bringing misfortune with them onto the Ark.

Don't shoot the albatross!

Immortalised by *The Rime of the Ancient Mariner* by Samuel Taylor Coleridge, everyone knows the age-old superstition that says it is terribly unlucky to kill an albatross. Anyone who kills one must wear the dead bird around their neck as a penance, which is the only thing that might protect the boat and crew from disaster. That's quite a penance, considering that the albatross is among the largest of flying birds, with the largest Great Albatross recorded as having a wingspan of over 11ft (about 3.5m). Though mainly found in Antarctica

and the southern Atlantic, as far north as the Cape of Good Hope, the albatross can fly great distances. They mate for life, but, living for fifty years or more, can spend years flying solitary. Obviously nobody's paid much attention to the superstition against killing them, though – 19 of the 21 species of albatross are on the endangered list.

The sight of a lone albatross, gliding around a ship and following her for days (as they are wont to do), must have made an impression on many sailors. Being followed by an albatross came to be seen as an omen of good luck, as if the albatross is making a protective gesture toward a vessel and her crew. However, pessimistic sailors saw this from the other angle – that they were in need of protection. So seeing an albatross can also be read as an omen of strong winds or bad weather ahead. Sailors believe it unlucky to kill an albatross because they host the immortal souls of dead seamen. As a nicer alternative to the Davy Jones's Locker theory (see page 57), when a sailor dies he turns into an albatross, allowing him to live forever at sea. Sailors see an albatross as one of their own, returned to watch over ship and crew. As D H Lawrence wrote: 'The dead don't die. They look on and help.'

Amongst the stories and rumours of misfortune that befell ships after someone on board killed an albatross, one that stands out is that of the *Calpean Star*, a cargo ship that sank in 1960. While docked in Liverpool late in 1959, fifty crew allegedly went on strike because the ship's cargo included an albatross destined for a zoo. En route to South America, one crewmember apparently fed it unsuitable food and it died. The ship soon suffered major engine failure and drifted for days.

Eventually reaching South Georgia, the ship ran onto rocks, which smashed her rudder and damaged one engine screw. She was towed to Montevideo, Uruguay for repairs, but upon leaving afterwards an explosion tore through her engine room and she sank in the River Plate. Though this might not be the fault of the albatross (or the sailor who killed it). The *Calpean Star* used to be called *Highland Chieftain*, and was renamed early in 1959 (see page 27).

Despite all this, it's actually something of a myth that sailors wouldn't kill an albatross. Indeed, they often ate them. As alluded to in Charles Baudelaire's poem, *L'Albatros* (from his collection *Les Fleurs du Mal*), idle sailors would catch the birds for sport. What's more, sailors sometimes had tobacco pouches made out of albatross feet, whilst traditionally, Maori tribesmen used albatross bones to scratch out ceremonial tattoos.

Other birds

Like the albatross, gulls were also believed to host the souls of sailors lost at sea, so it became similarly unlucky to kill them. Some sailors believe gulls own daylight, so killing one would strike its slayer blind. Gulls can be bad omens too. Three gulls flying together directly overhead is an omen of a death in the near future, whilst for the wives of sailors, or passengers on a ship, who live inland, seeing a gull can be a sign that there's bad weather out to sea.

Storm petrels, which come from the same order of seabirds as the albatross but look like a slightly less unfriendly gull, also foretell the weather. However, sailors read the sign in different ways. Some believe the appearance of a storm petrel (probably walking on water, as they are famous for doing) is a warning that bad weather is on the way. Others believe the storm petrel brings bad weather with it. Killing a storm petrel is also unlucky. On the other hand, as with an albatross, to be beneath a storm petrel when it answers a call of nature is supposedly lucky (unless the recipient standing below has no other clothes to change into).

A swallow, meanwhile, is good luck, but primarily because, as a land-based bird, its appearance tells a sailor he isn't far from shore. Naturally, killing one is bad luck. Birds that signify bad luck include crows, hawks and owls – especially if they land in the rigging. Cormorants and curlews can also be bad luck. A cormorant floating on the surface of the water without moving is a sign of bad weather coming, whilst sailors consider the faintly human cry of a curlew a warning from drowned friends.

Rats leaving a sinking ship

Unless they're carrying the plague, rats are not at all unlucky to have on board a boat. It's only if they leave that it's a bad sign. Sailors have long believed rats could sense disaster before it occurs, and that rats seen scurrying from a ship's hold before she sailed was a sure sign she would sink on her next voyage. There might be some truth to this. Rats lived in the dark corners of the hold, at the very bottom of the ship, so if she was taking on water, the rats would invariably be first to know about it.

In 1923 rats were supposedly seen fleeing the USS *Young* just before she left San Francisco in formation with thirteen other destroyers. What happened next became known as the Honda Point Disaster, and represents the largest loss of ships during peacetime in the history of the US Navy, before or since. Nine of the fourteen warships ran aground on rocks. Seven were lost. Of all the ships, the *Young* suffered the worst fate. The rocks tore her hull open, water rushed in, and she capsized in only a few minutes. In total, 23 sailors lost their lives at Honda Point – all but three of them were serving aboard the *Young*.

Cats (the one-tailed not nine-tailed variety)

Rats aren't the only animal that can tell when something bad is about to happen. In 1912 an Irish stoker due to sail to New York saw a black cat fleeing his ship, carrying her kittens off the liner in her mouth. Whilst black cats are unlucky on land, that's one of the many landlubber superstitions which are reversed at sea. Indeed, a black cat is the only black thing that isn't unlucky to have aboard a boat (see page 38). Conversely, white cats are very unlucky at sea, but a single white hair plucked from an otherwise all black cat can be considered a lucky charm. Though the Irish stoker's story can't be verified, he claimed seeing the cat leave the ship at Southampton convinced him to skip the job. If so, it was a decision he unlikely regretted – four days later the *Titanic* sank.

The Ancient Egyptians practiced a degree of cat worship, and the superstition against cats probably originated from the attempts of early Christians to wipe out these pagan beliefs. Sailors, meanwhile, came to see the cat as a bringer of luck. If a cat approached a sailor, the sailor considered that good luck. However, if the cat started to approach, but then changed direction, it took luck away with it, and the sailor could look forward to misfortune instead. Even worse for the sailor, if the cat crossed his path whilst walking away, he was probably doomed.

How a cat behaves can foretell the weather. A cat sneezing means rain, as does a cat lying on its ear, according to a German superstition. In New England, if a cat washes its face, the weather will come from whichever direction it's pointing at the time. Cats can also have a direct effect on the weather, so whilst they can bring luck to a voyage, they must be handled carefully and treated well. However tempting it might be in the middle of the night, when the ship's cat is using its claws to see which

crewmember will surrender his or her
berth to a sleepy feline first, never throw
a cat overboard. This will cause a storm.
Anyone who drowns a cat will invariably
end up drowning themselves, though an Irish
superstition says they will just have seventeen
years of bad luck instead. Never make a cat
(or let one become) angry – they carry wind
in their tails and a few aggravated twitches
could whip up a gale.

In small villages by the sea, cats were occasionally
stolen. Of course, the obvious culprit was the wife of
a sailor or fisherman, who would often want to keep a
cat at home to protect her husband whilst he was at sea. Seeing
as cats brought luck, the wives believed a cat would bring a sailor
home again safe.

Hogs, dogs and other animals

The era of the cavalry charge is long gone, so the need for navies
to transport horses overseas no longer exists. However, sailors of
modern yachts should be aware that it remains bad luck to have
a horse (or mule) that is white on board. Generally speaking,
though, as with people (like priests, see page 36), any animal not
at home on the water is considered unlucky to have at sea. This
means no dogs, and no pigs.

Despite being lucky to have as a tattoo (see page 31), pigs have
cloven hooves like the Devil. That pigs fear water and probably
kicked up an almighty stink the first time somebody tried to
take one on a boat invariably helped propagate the reputation
that they are bad luck at sea. Don't even mention a pig by name

(see page 55). Should a pig happen to be on board anyway, don't kill it – this will cause a storm.

The superstition against rabbits and hares at sea developed from a medieval landlubber suspicion that they were actually witches in disguise. Rabbits and hares can be unlucky even if they are dead, so don't take any leftover jugged hare or rabbit stew for lunch on the water. In the past, the most superstitious of captains (or those with the most superstitious of crews) might have decided to head back to port if they found signs of a rabbit or hare on board. They probably got their bad reputation from chewing through ropes on board. French fishermen, on the other hand, associated the notoriously fertile creatures with women (see page 33).

Not all animals are bad omens. A bee or butterfly landing on deck signifies good luck. Like swallows, these never fly too far from land. The more beautiful a sea creature is, the more luckier they are. Sea otters, flying fish and dolphins are good omens, for example, whilst sharks are bad ones. Though this doesn't explain why seals, which always draw affectionate coos from aquarium visitors, have a negative reputation for being reincarnations of the Pharaoh's army, drowned in the Red Sea whilst pursuing Moses and the Israelites.

Dolphins, sharks and rays

With dogs being unlucky at sea, dolphins are the sailor's best friend. They are famous for their fearlessness, approaching boats and playing around them, allowing people to feed them hand to mouth. A dolphin (or, even better, a pod of them) swimming with a boat blesses it with good luck. Fishermen (and many sailors) believe dolphins have the best interests of men at heart, so when there are some around, this means the boat is under their protection. Naturally, killing one is bad luck. This sterling reputation may have developed because the most friendly species of dolphin and porpoise live close to land, so they were a sign to a ship's crew that they were near the safety of port. Sailors can also use dolphin behaviour to forecast the weather. Seeing a dolphin swimming north means good weather is on the way, whilst seeing one swimming south signifies bad weather ahead.

Many consider it a Hollywood myth, but there are numerous accounts of dolphins protecting humans from shark attacks. Even dolphin experts are at a loss to explain why. Sometimes a lone dolphin will ram its nose into an attacking shark, but both a surfer injured by a Great White shark off the Californian coast in 2007 and a group of lifeguards who were attacked in New Zealand in 2004 reported an entire pod of dolphins forming a ring, swimming around them in circles so that the shark couldn't get through for another bite.

Unsurprisingly, then, a shark is a terrible omen. If one follows a boat that is a sign of an impending death. Just as they have highly attuned senses that can detect a single drop of blood in the ocean from miles away, sharks can supposedly sense those who are near death on a boat. Perhaps knowing how quickly those who die at sea were buried (see page 56), sharks came to expect a quick lunch. More likely is that sharks following a boat are just waiting for the remains of the crew's last meal, which are tossed overboard more often than bodies. Sharks will eat anything, from vegetable scraps to pieces of scrap metal. Sailors heading for waters where they know there to be sharks can always hang a preserved shark fin from the bowsprit. This acts as a warning to other sharks that they should keep away.

The manta ray is a strange-looking, unworldly creature which has also fallen foul of superstitious sailors, who call it the devilfish or sea devil instead. During the Age of Sail, crews of even the largest ships believed a manta ray could attach itself to the anchor and drag the ship underwater. With the largest rays growing to up to 25ft across, that's perhaps not surprising, though like several other reasonably harmless species the manta ray became more mythical monster than wonder of the deep.

Mermaids and other mythical beasts

Real animals aren't the limit of creatures considered lucky or unlucky, though for a long time sailors thought the likes of mermaids and sea serpents were just as real as dolphins. Nowadays it is assumed mermaids were created in the imaginations of nervy sailors who spotted sea lions or manatees at a distance or in a half light. It's mostly Disney's fault that the popular image of this half-fish woman is a delightful girl frolicking in the waves. Sailors certainly would have preferred that. The mermaid myth owes more to the sirens of Greek mythology – the beautiful women who lured ships onto the rocks with their wonderful singing voices. Mermaids were bad.

In 1901 the Royal Navy frigate HMS *Daedalus* was on its way to St Helena from the Cape of Good Hope when the Officer on Watch spotted something in the water about two hundred yards away. To be sure he wasn't just imagining it he summoned other officers and crew, but even Captain McQuhae later corroborated what they saw to *The Times*. The sea serpent was about sixty feet long, though some of those on the *Daedalus* said it resembled a lizard more than a snake. The Admiralty (as well as several Members of Parliament) reacted with outrage when the story was reported seriously by *The Times*, believing it brought the Royal Navy into ridicule. After all, what seems rational in the lonely waters of the South Seas might seem a little silly in the London suburbs. As with the Loch Ness Monster, sea serpent sightings usually depend upon the iceberg principle: a little is seen above the water and the imagination fills in the rest. Whilst the crew of the *Daedalus* estimated the sea serpent was some sixty feet long, they only saw a few feet of its head: a large mouth, nose and some fins. Most likely it was a whale.

Similarly, the giant squid probably gave rise to the kraken legend. Female giant squid can reach almost 45ft (about 14m) – a truly imposing sight if one appears out of the depths beside a vessel. According to myth, the kraken is a giant octopus that surfaces directly beneath its target vessel then reaches its many legs around, crushing the hull and stealing men off the deck. Anything left behind is supposedly sucked down by the whirlpool left in the kraken's wake as it descends into the depths with its prey. Of course, as with other such stories of zero survival, there is a sizeable plothole in the fact that if any of it was true, there would have been nobody left to report it.

Food and Fishing

During the Age of Sail the Royal Navy served food to the men on its ships in square wooden plates with round hollows (called trenchers) which were designed not to roll around on tables in rough seas. The phrase 'square meal' is sometimes attributed to the fact that basic rations usually only filled the round hollow, but if a sailor was given a hearty amount the food would fill the square part too. This is probably untrue, as use of the word 'square' to mean good and true goes back a lot further, and appears in Shakespeare. However, the edges of these square plates were supposedly called fiddles, and a sailor who took more than his ration would have food 'on the fiddle'.

Meat packed into wooden cases with salt to preserve it for months (or even longer); water turned green (from being kept in slimy barrels) used to dilute rum, wine and beer; British seamen sucking on sour limes (hence the national nickname, 'limeys') to stave off scurvy – the sailor's diet used to deserve its terrible reputation. Things have come a long way since ships' biscuits which contained extra protein in the form of live weevil larvae, but those who go to sea must still be careful about food. If possible, sailors should catch their own. After all, nothing tastes better than fresh fish that only takes a matter of minutes to get from sea to plate.

Should a sailor find a maggot in his cookie today, he might want to bear in mind a superstition that recommends throwing the cook overboard to help quell a storm. Alternatively, if a fish supper is cooked to perfection, throw the cook's boot overboard instead (preferably the left one, see page 43).

Bananas

The worst food of all to bring to a picnic on the poop deck is a banana. Bananas have a terrible reputation amongst sailors, to the extent that in parts of Florida and Hawaii some consider not only the name and image but also the colour yellow unlucky. The fruit has been considered bad luck since before the eighteenth century, but that's when countless stories began to spread of ships (predominantly Spanish) disappearing in the western Atlantic with holds full of bananas. There are a myriad of theories, some more outlandish than others, as to how the banana got a bad name in the first place.

Besides supernatural forces in the Bermuda Triangle (see page 61), the most outlandish theory – which is more of a legend, really – involves a slave transport ship that was carrying a cargo of bananas in the hold. The bananas started to rot quickly in the heat of the Caribbean, and the fruit juices fermented, releasing methane gas. The gas built up in the hold, killing all the slaves. Different versions of the same theory diverge here. In one version the gas reached a combustible level and caused the ship to explode. In a more popular version the ship didn't explode, but the crew succumbed to gas poisoning, allowing the story to become a classic tale of a ship found adrift with the crew all dead. The problem with this version is that methane isn't toxic – though it can cause asphyxiation if it displaces enough oxygen.

Another sort of theory blames the banana's bad reputation variously on spiders, scorpions or snakes. Apparently a certain species of deadly spider (or scorpion, or snake) hides amongst the leaves of bunches of bananas. When crewmen suddenly died after bananas were brought on board, the fruit got the blame, but really they had received lethal bites or stings from venomous critters. There might be something to this theory, in that those loading (or unloading) crates of bananas could get bitten or stung, which would make ships carrying bananas unlucky with both sailors and stevedores. However, most spider bites and scorpion stings are painful rather than lethal, and noticeable for what they are, so the banana couldn't be blamed for ship disappearances. That didn't stop fanciful stories spreading of ships being overrun by spiders hiding amongst bananas multiplying and killing everyone on board. Snakes, too, are reasonably blameless, because most of the species that live in the parts of the world where bananas grow tend to be constrictors that suffocate their prey rather than poison them. In fact, the only animal that could be brought on board in a crate of bananas which might prove lethal for the entire crew is a rat infected with the plague, or carrying ticks infected with typhus (see page 56).

However, the most plausible theory as to why bananas got a bad name is also the least interesting. In the days before refrigeration, the ships transporting bananas from the Tropics to ports along the eastern seaboard of the United States only had a limited time to get them there before the fruit started to go off. So only the fastest ships could do this job. These ships went so fast, in fact, that it was impossible for the crew to fish over the side. Naturally, the banana got the blame. Sailors convinced themselves fish don't like them. Today some fishermen maintain fish won't bite if they have eaten a banana, got banana oil on their hand, which then gets on the bait.

At the table

Bananas aren't the only food that shouldn't be taken on board, but with others it's more a case of taking care when eating them. Don't eat walnuts on a boat, for the same reason walnut wood should not be used in a boat's construction (see page 8). Avoid pea soup, too. Nowadays sailors believe it's called 'storm soup' because it calls up a storm, but it got the name originally because in rough weather ships' cooks would only use one pot in the galley, and throw everything into it. Best not to tempt fate, though. Think carefully before taking eggs on board. Some sailors believe eggs can turn the wind against them. Those who decide to risk it and have a boiled egg for lunch must remember to make a hole in the bottom of the shell after eating it. It was a common belief that witches used egg shells to sail across the sea.

Be careful when cutting bread. Don't turn the loaf upside down (and especially don't leave it standing like that) as this anticipates the boat capsizing. Upturning a teapot to empty it invokes the same thing. Similarly, don't open a tin can from the bottom, and always hang coffee or tea cups so that their mouths face the hull. Don't stir drinks with a knife or fork, and never stir anything counter clockwise. Don't cross knives on the galley table. And never pass any salt between those seated. Remember the saying: Pass salt, pass sorrow.

Despite all the important uses for whiskey already described, some captains won't allow anyone to bring any on board their vessel, let alone drink any, insisting that it is a landlubber's drink, and that sailors should drink rum instead. After the whiskey plank fitting, christening, launching and setting sail, most sailors would be lucky to have any left in the bottle anyway. Regardless of what a sailor drinks, he should always give the first tot to the sea.

Bad luck fishing

If fishing is poor, it may be because there's a scutcher on board – an unlucky item that drives the fish away. To begin with, check through the list of contraband on page 38. However, the fish might not bite if the fisherman broke any of the following rules. As with everything else, never fish on a Friday (see page 45). Don't bother trying to catch any fish when the wind is coming from the east or north (though some say the west and south instead – perhaps it depends upon which hemisphere). Cast lines or nets over the starboard side (probably because this is what Jesus Christ recommended to his future disciples on the Sea of Galilee). If using lines, don't sit too closely to someone else. Fish won't bite on crossed lines. They also won't come to someone who swears whilst fishing.

Never count any fish until the end of the day – a fisherman who counts his fish would be considered covetous by the sea, which might refuse to provide any more. Don't taste any food before the first fish is caught, but once a fish is caught and eaten, don't burn its bones, and don't wash its guts or scales from boots or the deck. Luck will be washed away too. If a Scottish fisherman caught a left boot by mistake he would spit on it and then throw it back. A left boot is unlucky (see page 43). However, catching a right boot is good luck. Nail it to the mast to bring good fortune to the vessel. Finally, the fisherman who finds a spot that rewards him with plenty of fish shouldn't tell anyone about it. The sea is very picky about who receives the bounty of its generosity.

Good luck fishing

Some of the things a fisherman can do to ensure a good catch need to be done before he even leaves shore. At the start of the fishing season, for example, salt in the nets (see page 30), and shed a few drops of blood in a fight – though be careful not to get any in the water (see page 53). Scottish fishermen clearly didn't believe in the superstition which warns that once the sea gets a taste of someone it will be hungry for more; on reaching the fishing spot, they used to throw one member of the crew overboard then haul him back in, in the belief this would make the fish follow suit.

Whilst poor weather is bad for sailors, some fishermen consider a cloudy or rainy day good for fishing. Indeed, some even believe thunder brings fish to the surface. The direction of the wind can also indicate how good the fishing will be, so if the wind changes direction, take that as a sign either way. The easy way to remember is with the rhyme: Wind from the south, hook in the mouth. Wind from the east, bite the least. Wind from the north, further off. Wind from the west, bite the best.

If fishing with a line, spit on the bait for good luck. Some fishermen believe in spitting on the first fish caught and then throwing it back, but others say throwing the first fish back is tantamount to throwing away luck, and that it will be the last fish caught. Those who subscribe to the latter superstition should present the first fish to the master of the vessel (whether that's the boat's owner, the captain or just dad) to eat. He should be sure to eat it from head to tail. If he starts at the tail it will have time to warn other fish, and no more will be caught on that trip.

If All Else Fails

If a sailor breaks one of the superstitions in this book, he has a brief opportunity to escape misfortune. Landlubbers who realise they have done or said something which tempts fate often say 'Touch wood' (or 'Knock on wood').

Of course, touching wood to escape misfortune isn't very helpful to a sailor who has a modern fibreglass yacht. The sailor's alternative is to touch iron instead of wood. Shoes used to have iron nails in them, but sailors could also touch an iron ring or bolt, or a horseshoe nailed to the mast (see page 43). Iron is heavy, and used even less than wood in modern boats, so touching iron isn't necessarily a very helpful suggestion either. Fortunately, as with wood, a sailor can invoke the act simply by saying 'Cold iron'. Maybe twice, just to be safe.

At the end of the day, nothing in this book will protect the unprepared sailor. Sailors invented superstitions as a way to try and influence or control what was actually uncontrollable. Many of those uncontrollable things remain uncontrollable today, regardless of the advances made in maritime technology and forecasting the weather. Nowadays we also seem to have replaced many superstitions with health and safety rules. But that book wouldn't have been quite so much fun to read.

Index